In this relatively short book, Tim Cl
comprehensively key issues about w
a crucial role in a growing relationsl
probably be helpful to mull over eac
ideas into practice as you read the Bible. The areas covered in this
book will help to enrich your encounter with God as you engage
with his word.
Elaine Duncan, Chief Executive, Scottish Bible Society

Tim answers a lot of common questions, speaks to a lot of
common issues and most of all helps us to see how the most
important voice in the universe speaks to us in the Bible. This
is more than useful – it's inspiring.
Julian Hardyman, Senior Pastor, Eden Baptist Church, Cambridge

Tim Chester is one of the clearest, most useful and reliable
Christian writers in the UK today. This book on the Bible will
encourage and reassure you and answer many questions. Tim is
widely and deeply read yet he writes with great accessibility and
pastoral sensitivity, coming alongside the reader to instruct and
to apply his teaching to life in the modern world.
*Peter Lewis, author, conference speaker and former Senior Pastor
of Cornerstone Church, Nottingham*

Inspirational, profound, realistic. In ten easy-to-read yet
informative chapters and using immensely practical examples,
Tim Chester shows how we can approach the Bible so that, when
we read it or hear it preached, we can hear the voice of God who
refreshes our souls and makes us wise. If you can buy only one
book on the Bible, buy this one!
*Tricia Marnham, Bible teacher and Director of Women's Ministry,
St Michael's, Chester Square, London*

I am delighted to commend Tim Chester's *Bible Matters*, the latest addition to the Keswick Foundations series. I've been encouraged and taught by it as I've read it. I appreciated the comprehensive yet accessible coverage, the merging of the historical, theological, personal and applied; the turns of phrase, the clarity and the imagery. The most striking insight for me is that the Bible is 'weird' and not the kind of book that we would write because its purpose is not simply to give *information about* God but to develop our *relationship with* God. But there are many more [such insights]. Buy, read, recommend, lend, give away!
James Robson, Ministry Director, Keswick Ministries

BIBLE
MATTERS

BIBLE MATTERS

Meeting God in his word

TIM CHESTER

INTER-VARSITY PRESS
36 Causton Street, London SW1P 4ST, England
Email: ivp@ivpbooks.com
Website: www.ivpbooks.com

First published 2017

British Library Cataloguing-in-Publication Data
A catalogue record for this book is available from the British Library.

ISBN: 978–1–78359–579–2
eBook ISBN: 978–1–78359–580–8

Set in Dante 12/15 pt
Typeset in Great Britain by CRB Associates, Potterhanworth, Lincolnshire
Printed in Great Britain by Ashford Colour Press Ltd, Gosport, Hampshire

*Inter-Varsity Press publishes Christian books that are true to the Bible and that
communicate the gospel, develop discipleship and strengthen the church for its mission
in the world.*

*IVP originated within the Inter-Varsity Fellowship, now the Universities and Colleges
Christian Fellowship, a student movement connecting Christian Unions in universities
and colleges throughout Great Britain, and a member movement of the International
Fellowship of Evangelical Students. Website: www.uccf.org.uk. That historic association
is maintained, and all senior IVP staff and committee members subscribe to the UCCF
Basis of Faith.*

Contents

Keswick Foundations: Series preface

Our prayer was for deep, clear, powerful teaching,
which would take hold of the souls of the people,
and overwhelm them, and lead them to a full,
definite and all-conquering faith in Jesus.

This simple but profound prayer, expressed by Thomas
Harford-Battersby as he reported on the 1880 Keswick Convention, explains why hundreds of thousands of Christians the
world over have been committed to the Keswick movement.
The *purpose* is nothing other than to see believers more whole-
heartedly committed to Jesus Christ in every area of life,
and the *means* the faithful, clear and relevant exposition of
God's Word.

All around the world, the Keswick movement has this
purpose and this means. Whether it is to proclaim the gospel,
to encourage discipleship, to call for holiness, to urge for
mission, to long for the Spirit's empowering or to appeal
for unity – hearing God's Word in Scripture is central to fulfilling these priorities. More information about Keswick
Ministries is found at the end of this book.

Keswick Foundations is a series of books which introduce
the priority themes that have shaped the Keswick movement,
themes which we believe continue to be essential for the
church today. By God's grace, for 140 years the movement has
had an impact across the globe, not only through Conventions

large and small, but also through a range of media. Books in the Keswick Foundations series provide biblical, accessible and practical introductions to basic evangelical essentials that are vital for every Christian and every local church.

Our prayer for these books is the same as that expressed by Harford-Battersby – that by his Spirit, God's Word will take hold of our souls, leading us to an all-conquering faith in Jesus Christ, which will send us out to live and work for his glory.

Introduction

Let me tell you about an amazing experience I had just this morning. Actually 'amazing' doesn't really do it justice. It was out of this world.

This morning God spoke to me. I know that sounds weird, but I'm sure that's what happened. The living God actually spoke to me. I could hear what he was saying just as clearly as you can understand what you're reading now.

The words he spoke felt like words of life to me. They resounded deep in my heart. There were words of instruction that helped me know him more and understand his ways. There were words of challenge that called me to follow him better and love him more. There were words of comfort that spoke to my needs and gave me hope. It was like medicine to my soul. It was like a rousing speech before battle. It was like a love song sung to my heart.

What's more, what happened to me this morning was not a freaky one-off experience. It's what happens most mornings.

What I did this morning was read my Bible.

At this point you might be feeling like I've just pulled a fast one on you (unless, of course, you saw it coming a mile off).

You were hoping for a dramatic story, and what you got instead was daily Bible reading. 'Boring!'

My number one aim for this book is this: I want you to realize that every time you read the Bible, you're hearing the voice of God – just as surely, more surely, than if you have some kind of dramatic experience. I want you to come to the Bible, whether you're hearing it preached on a Sunday morning or reading it on the bus on a Monday morning, with a sense of anticipation and expectancy. Reading the Bible is a dramatic Spirit-filled experience. The God who spoke and brought the universe into existence speaks to you. The God whose voice thundered from Mount Sinai speaks to you. The God in Christ whose words healed the sick speaks to you.

I've read lots of things about the Bible that I've agreed with. But very few have captured how I *feel* about the Bible and *why*. That's what I've tried to do in this book. Its central premise is that the Bible is an *intentional* book. God gave it to us with a purpose in mind, and that purpose is to enter into, and live in, a relationship with his people. So the Bible is also a *relational* book. As we read it, we don't merely learn information about God – though that's certainly true. We hear God's voice and encounter his presence. This is a book about meeting God in his word.

I read my Bible regularly because I have to. Not 'have to' in the sense that someone might tell me off if I don't or that God will get miffed with me. But 'have to' in the same way that I have to eat food every day. This is how I live. Without God's word in my life, I too readily get preoccupied with myself, my fears, my insecurities, my reputation. Without God's word, I'm so much more vulnerable to temptation. I need God's word to realign my heart day by day towards Jesus. I need that medicine for the soul, that battle speech, that love song.

1

The God who speaks

Tell me about the book you're reading.

You're only a few words in, but you already know a fair bit about it. You know it's about the Bible – the title is a bit of a giveaway. You might remember the author and publisher. You probably read the blurb on the back cover. Maybe you ran your eyes over the contents page. At some point you examined it – perhaps in the shop when you bought it or when someone gave it to you. If you ordered it online, then maybe you read some customer reviews. You can see it and feel it. Some people like the smell of new books, so you may even have sniffed it . . . now most of you have. After you've read a couple of chapters you'll have an idea whether you like it or not. And if you make it to the end, you'll be able to tell other people about it in an informed way.

It's easy to examine a book and find out about it. You can investigate it and interrogate it.

Now, I don't want to alarm you, but there are almost certainly some bacteria on your book. If it's any comfort, they were probably transferred on to the book (or e-reader) from your hands. Can you tell me about the bacteria on your book? That's not so straightforward. You can't see, hear or feel them. Hopefully you can't smell them either, and I don't recommend trying to taste them. Nevertheless, with a powerful microscope or some chemical tests, you could find out something about them. Like a book, they're susceptible to scrutiny.

What about God? Tell me about God.

You might have all sorts of ideas about God. But upon what are they based? You can't see God through a telescope or under a microscope. You can't go and knock on his door to ask him some questions. You can't discover him in the jungle or on the ocean floor. He's not like other subjects of study. He's not susceptible to scrutiny.

For one thing, he's a spirit. He has no body and therefore no physical presence. Even more significantly, he's outside our universe. The Large Hadron Collider in Switzerland is the world's largest machine and largest experiment feeding results into the largest network of computers. The irony of all these superlatives is that it's designed to detect the smallest things we know about – subatomic particles. It's detecting the after-effects of particle collisions. But no apparatus could be constructed to 'find' God, because God doesn't exist within our material world. What would our experiment look for? In 2012 the Hadron Collider found evidence for the Higgs boson, a particle which had previously only been postulated. It was nicknamed 'the God particle'. But it wasn't a 'piece' of God or evidence of his existence.

God is beyond our comprehension and outside our field of study. We might postulate his existence as the most likely explanation of effects we can see – things like the complexity of creation or answers to prayer. But we could never prove our hypothesis. We can't stick God under a microscope or in a test tube.

So left to ourselves, we would remain totally in the dark when it comes to God. We have no way of bridging the gap between us and God.

So my request that you tell me about God should be an impossible task. The only way we can ever know anything about him is if he communicates to us. God himself must bridge the gap. We can't study him. But maybe he can talk to us.

And God is not silent.

Knowing God is not completely without parallel in our world. Suppose I said, 'Tell me about yourself.' Here's a subject you do know something about. In fact, arguably you're better informed on this topic than anyone else. The more you tell me about yourself, the more I'll know about you.

But wait a moment. Do you really want to spill the beans to me? After all, we've only just met. It's up to you what you tell me. How much I discover about your dreams, hopes, ideas, beliefs, desires and plans all depends on how much you tell me. I can't control what information comes my way. Only torturers can force information from people, and even then the reliability of that information is doubtful. In this sense the speaker is sovereign when we communicate.

It's the same with God. We can know about him because he speaks to us. But God remains in control of the process. We talk about 'grasping' an idea. But we don't 'grasp' God – not even when he reveals himself.

How does God talk to us?

1. God talks to us in creation

We can't see God. But we can see what he's done. We can see the impact he's made. And we don't have to look very far. Everything that exists points to God. Psalm 19 begins:

The heavens declare the glory of God;
   the skies proclaim the work of his hands.
Day after day they pour forth speech;
   night after night they reveal knowledge.
They have no speech, they use no words;
   no sound is heard from them.
Yet their voice goes out into all the earth,
   their words to the ends of the world.
(Psalm 19:1–4)

The skies pour forth speech. They're like an excited friend whom you can't shut up. From subatomic particles to vast galaxies, from intricate petals to stunning landscapes, the world is constantly declaring God's glory.

Creation doesn't tell us all we need to know about God. But it tells us some important things. Romans 1:20 says, 'For since the creation of the world God's invisible qualities – his eternal power and divine nature – have been clearly seen, being understood from what has been made, so that people are without excuse.' God speaks through creation of his 'eternal power and divine nature'.

It doesn't add up to a QED moment for sceptics. Atheists and agnostics have seen a sunset and still they doubt God's existence.

Maybe you've looked out at a beautiful scene or watched some astonishing nature footage on the television and said something like, 'How can people not believe in God when they see this?' But sceptics are not blind or stupid. The problem is not that they're looking in the other direction. They're not standing at a viewpoint focused on overflowing rubbish bins while you look at the beautiful scenery. It's not that they think flowers and sunsets and birdsong are ugly. The problem is a moral one. People 'suppress the truth by their wickedness'

(Romans 1:18). We'll meet this theme a number of times in our exploration of the Bible and come back to it in the final chapter. We find reasons for discounting the evidence before our eyes because we don't want to live with the implications of being accountable to God or dependent on him.

But just because we're not listening doesn't mean God's not talking.

The psalmist says,

Day after day they pour forth speech;
    night after night they reveal knowledge.
(Psalm 19:2)

All the time, day and night, everywhere we go, the world speaks of God's power and goodness.

Sometimes small children cover their eyes to 'make it go away'. It's as if what they can't see can't be seen. Humanity is like this. We cover our ears to God's voice in creation as if what we can't hear can't be there:

Yet their voice goes out into all the earth,
    their words to the ends of the world.
(Psalm 19:4)

When we become a Christian, God removes our hands from our ears. Suddenly everything speaks of God. Now we're able to see his glory in the world. We hear God speaking through creation loud and clear. And what we see and hear is marvellous. The hymnwriter George Robinson put it like this:

Heav'n above is softer blue,
Earth around is sweeter green!

Something lives in every hue
Christless eyes have never seen;
Birds with gladder songs o'erflow,
Flowers with deeper beauties shine,
Since I know, as now I know,
I am his, and he is mine.[1]

The world comes alive to us in this way because now we see it as a gift from the Creator. We hear his voice speaking of his glory.

2. God talks to us in history

If you'd asked an ancient Israelite to tell you about God, they would have told you a story – the story of the exodus.

At the beginning of the exodus story, Moses encounters God in the burning bush at Mount Horeb. There God reveals his name to Moses: 'I AM WHO I AM'. But it's the rest of the story that gives this declaration content. Moses imagines the Israelites asking him who it is who has sent him to liberate them. 'What is his name?' they will ask. Who is this God who claims to be our God? In response, God not only declares I AM WHO I AM; he also promises to perform wonders among the Egyptians (Exodus 3:13–22). In other words, the ultimate answer to the question of God's identity is the exodus itself. God speaks through the exodus:

To his people: 'I will take you as my own people, and I will be your God. Then you will know that I am the LORD your God, who brought you out from under the yoke of the Egyptians' (Exodus 6:7).

To the Egyptians: 'Then I will lay my hand on Egypt and with mighty acts of judgment I will bring out my divisions, my people the Israelites. And the Egyptians will know that I am the LORD when I stretch out my hand against Egypt and bring the Israelites out of it' (Exodus 7:4–5).

To all nations: 'For by now I could have stretched out my hand and struck you and your people with a plague that would have wiped you off the earth. But I have raised you up for this very purpose, that I might show you my power and that my name might be proclaimed in all the earth' (Exodus 9:15–16).

Through the exodus God spoke to all people of his grace, power and judgment. Again and again in the Bible, God speaks through the way he intervenes in history.

But it's not just events recorded in the Bible through which God speaks. The events of *all* human history reveal God. The events of your life reveal God. If you're a child of God, they're signs of God's provision for you. If you're not a Christian, then they're God's invitations and warnings to you.

Romans 1:18 says, 'The wrath of God is being revealed from heaven against all the godlessness and wickedness of people, who suppress the truth by their wickedness.' Right now God is communicating his wrath to the world. How? Three times in Romans 1 it says that God hands people over to sin (1:24, 26, 28):

- 'God gave them over in the sinful desires.'
- 'God gave them over to shameful lusts.'
- 'God gave them over to a depraved mind.'

Often God in his mercy restrains the effects of sin. But sometimes he lets sin take its course. He allows it to follow its natural downward bent towards death. He does this to expose the ugly reality of sin and reveal his coming judgment. As a result, we see unnatural sex, wickedness, evil, greed, depravity, envy, murder, strife, deceit, malice and so on (1:26–31). Our instinctive sense that these things are wrong and don't belong in our world points to a higher moral standard set by a higher moral Being (Romans 2:15).

Revelation 8 – 9 describes the chaos of history – environmental catastrophe, natural disasters, war. They're described as 'plagues' (9:18). It's an echo of the exodus story. The plagues on Egypt revealed God to the Egyptians. The calamities of history are intended to reveal God to humanity. But like the beauty of creation, humanity refuses to listen. Revelation 9:20 says, 'The rest of mankind who were not killed by these plagues still did not repent of the work of their hands.' But again, the fact that we're not listening doesn't mean God isn't talking.

3. God talks to us in his Son

This is one example of God speaking in history. He speaks in the historical event of the incarnation. But this is an event that eclipses all others. That's because in Jesus the triune God reveals himself not just in an event, but in a person. And not just in person, but a person who is God: God revealed in God.

Hebrews 1:1–2 says, 'In the past God spoke to our ancestors through the prophets at many times and in various ways, but in these last days he has spoken to us by his Son, whom he appointed heir of all things, and through whom he made the universe.' It's literally: 'He has spoken to us in a Son.' He's spoken in the language of Son. There are lots of jokes about the language of heaven. But here's the reality: the language in which God speaks is Jesus. God's fullest revelation of himself is Jesus. When God opens his mouth to speak, as it were, Jesus is what comes out.

Hebrews continues, 'The Son is the radiance of God's glory and the exact representation of his being' (1:3). The Son is the revelation of God not just in history, but eternally. He is the eternal Word of God who was with God in the beginning (John 1:1–3). Eternally, the Son has been the image of God, the perfect mirror of the Father's glory.

Suppose I write to you and say, 'Tell me about yourself.' You could write a letter describing your appearance and your character. But a much better option would be to come to see me. That's why employers want to interview prospective job applicants and not just read a CV. You only really know a person by seeing them, hearing them, spending time with them. God has sent us a letter or a CV. That's what the Bible is. But he did so much more. He turned up in person – in the person of his Son, Jesus. Do you want to know what God is like? Look at Jesus because Jesus is God. Jesus is the definition of who God is that God himself has given us.

4. God talks to us in the Bible

It must have been great to see Jesus walk on water, heal the sick, preach to the crowds, rise again – God's ultimate revelation standing before your very eyes with his words ringing in your ears.

But what about us today? Jesus has ascended into heaven. So we can no longer see him or hear him. How does God speak to people now? Think about how that question was answered in the generation following the ascension of Jesus. How did the first Christians know about Jesus? The answer, of course, is that there were people around who had seen and heard Jesus. They could give a first-hand eyewitness account of God's revelation in Jesus. The apostle John's first letter begins:

That which was from the beginning, which we have heard, which we have seen with our eyes, which we have looked at

and our hands have touched – this we proclaim concerning the Word of life. The life appeared; we have seen it and testify to it, and we proclaim to you the eternal life, which was with the Father and has appeared to us. We proclaim to you what we have seen and heard, so that you also may have fellowship with us. And our fellowship is with the Father and with his Son, Jesus Christ.
(1 John 1:1–3)

John basically says the same thing three times:

verse 1 = we proclaim what we have seen
verse 2 = we proclaim what we have seen
verse 3 = we proclaim what we have seen

What is it that has been seen and is proclaimed? It's 'the Word of life'. He's talking about Jesus. John is echoing the language at the beginning of his Gospel: 'In the beginning was the Word . . . The Word became flesh . . . We have seen his glory . . .' (John 1:1, 14). But John is also echoing *the end* of his Gospel. When Thomas hears that Jesus has risen, he says, 'Unless I see the nail marks in his hands and put my finger where the nails were, and put my hand into his side, I will not believe.' And then Jesus meets Thomas and says, 'Put your finger here; see my hands. Reach out your hand and put it into my side. Stop doubting and believe' (John 20:25–27). Jesus said, 'See my hands', and now John says, 'We have seen.' Jesus said, 'Reach out your hand', and now John says, 'Our hands have touched.' That's why John calls the Word 'the Word of life'. The Word he saw, heard and touched had risen from the dead.

But the important question to ask about these verses is who are the 'we' that John keeps talking about? In these first four verses John refers to 'we', 'our' or 'us' sixteen times. He's not talking about 'we Christians'. He's not including you and me. For one thing, you and I didn't see, hear and touch the risen Jesus. Plus John talks about 'we' in contrast to 'you', his readers. 'We proclaim to you what we have seen and heard, so that you also may have fellowship with us' (1 John 1:3). The 'we' are the first apostles, those who were there.

How do we have contact with God's revelation in Jesus? We have the testimony of the apostles – the people on the spot who heard, saw and touched Jesus. This is what Paul means when he says in Ephesians 2:20 that the church is built on the foundation of the apostles and prophets. Christ himself left no written record, so, says B. B. Warfield, 'We have no Christ except the one whom the apostles have given us.'[2]

'Well, that's great for you, John,' you might be tempted to say. 'But I'm never going to touch Jesus.' But John continues in 1 John 1:4: 'We write this to make our joy complete.' We have the apostolic testimony because they wrote it down. We have their testimony about the Word of life in the Bible – along with the promises of the prophets in the Old Testament.

Imagine there's no Bible. The first apostles know about the message of salvation and they start telling people. And people tell people who tell people. That, after all, is essentially how the message of Christianity has spread. But without the Bible, Chinese whispers might kick in. Chinese whispers is when you whisper a sentence to someone who whispers it to someone else and so on round the room. Inevitably, it gets distorted – hopefully to comic effect. But what if the gospel got twisted and distorted as it made its way around the globe and across the centuries? That would not be to comic effect. Memories fade. Stories get distorted in retelling. Interpretations of history differ. So God has ensured an accurate record of his actions in history and an authoritative interpretation of those events. The Bible means there's a fixed point to which the proclamation of the gospel always returns. No-one can distort it very much before people start to spot the difference.

The seventeenth-century theologian Francis Turretin gives three reasons why God's revelation was written down. First, to protect it against 'the weakness of memory'. If the gospel had relied on oral transmission, then mistakes might have crept in. Second, so it might be 'defended from the frauds and corruptions of Satan'. False claims can readily be tested against Scripture. Third, so it could 'more conveniently . . . be sent to the absent and . . . transmitted to posterity'.[3] Without the Bible, we would be reliant on hearsay. With the Bible, we all have access to the voice of God.

5. God talks to us in preaching

Have you ever said, 'God really spoke to me through Sunday's sermon'? I'm sure you have. Is that simply a metaphorical way of saying you found the sermon challenging or encouraging? I think not. God really does continue to speak to his people through other human beings. This revelation, however, is not on the same level as the Bible. The Bible, as we shall see, is entirely trustworthy. Human beings are not. We often speak the truth. But we also often get that truth muddled up with the lies of this world and our own self-justifications. So the Bible is always the final standard of truth. Nevertheless, God uses other people to speak to our hearts.

Talking about his preaching among the Thessalonians, Paul says, 'When you received the word of God, which you heard from us, you accepted it not as a human word, but as it actually is, the word of God, which is indeed at work in you who believe' (1 Thessalonians 2:13). Paul isn't talking about a time when the Thessalonians read the Bible. He's talking about how they heard his preaching. It looked like a human word. But actually it was God's word being spoken by a human being.

The apostle Peter speaks of 'those who have preached the gospel to you by the Holy Spirit sent from heaven' (1 Peter 1:12). The Holy Spirit is sent from heaven to enable preachers. Of course, some preachers can distort the message and give people merely what they want to hear (2 Timothy 4:3). That's why the Bible is always the touchstone of truth. But it's also true that God can speak through preachers 'by the Holy Spirit sent from heaven'. Peter says the Spirit has given some people in the church the gift of speaking the truth we find in the Bible into the contexts of their hearers. He says, 'If anyone speaks, they should do so as one who speaks the very words of God' (1 Peter 4:11). It's a bold statement. If preachers are being true to the Bible, then they're speaking 'the very words of God'. If friends are encouraging you with truth from the Bible, then they're speaking 'the very words of God'.

When the Bible is taught or preached or read or explained or sung, or when people exhort us or encourage us using the Bible, then God's voice can be heard. It's not heard infallibly – only the Bible is infallible. Every word of the Bible is inspired. Uniquely so. But to the extent that people correctly communicate the message of the Bible, God uses them to speak to us.

The New Testament speaks of the gift of prophecy and words of knowledge. Some Christians believe the Holy Spirit continues to give these gifts to people in the church. Other Christians believe these gifts have ceased because we no longer need prophecy now that the New Testament is complete.

Whatever we think about this issue, we need to be clear that this gift of prophecy is not like Old Testament prophecy. Paul says the church is 'built on the foundation of the apostles and prophets' (Ephesians 2:20). The contemporary equivalent of Old Testament prophecy is the apostolic testimony recorded in the New Testament. Old Testament prophets and New Testament apostles brought God's authoritative word to his people. In contrast, prophecy in the New Testament was to be weighed (1 Thessalonians 5:19–22).

I believe prophecy involves bringing God's word to bear in a particular situation. So it's *intimately tied to God's word in the Bible* and involves applying that word to specific situations. I think the primary way that happens is in the preaching of the church. Indeed, the Puritans often spoke of preaching as prophesying. In the sixteenth century the Puritan William Perkins wrote a preaching manual which he called *The Art of Prophesying*. Maybe you've had moments when it felt like the preacher was speaking just to you. Sometimes people jokingly accuse me of preparing a sermon with them in mind. (I'm always tempted to say that, surprising as it might seem, I don't think about them all the time.) Sometimes in pastoral situations someone has a 'hunch' about what the real issue may be. I don't really mind whether you call this prophecy or not. But I do think we should expect God to speak through human beings, always remembering that the truth will be an application of the truth we find in the Bible.

The Second Helvetic Confession of the Swiss Reformed Church says,

> Wherefore when this Word of God is now preached in the church by preachers lawfully called, we believe that *the very Word of God is proclaimed, and received by the faithful*; and that neither any other Word of God is to be invented nor is to be expected from heaven: and that now the Word itself which is preached is to be regarded, not the minister that preaches; for even if he be evil and a sinner, nevertheless the Word of God remains still true and good.[4]

The Reformer Martin Luther says, 'People generally think: "If I had an opportunity to hear God speak in person, I would run my feet bloody" . . . But you now have the Word of God in church . . . and this is God's Word as surely as if God Himself were speaking to you.'[5] Or John Calvin says, 'Christ acts by [his ministers] in such a manner that he wishes their *mouth* to be reckoned as his *mouth*, and their *lips* as his *lips*; that is, when they speak from his mouth, and faithfully declare his word.'[6]

So let me encourage you to treasure the preaching of God's word by preparing for it and following it up. The Puritan William Perkins advised, 'To the profitable hearing of God's Word three things are required: Preparation before we hear, a right disposition in hearing, and duties to be practised afterward.' By preparation, he meant three things. First, repenting of sin so that our hearts are unclouded by selfish thoughts. Second, praying that God would give us 'the Hearing ear' to understand and submit to God's word. Third, 'the hearer must set himself in the presence of God . . . because God is always in the congregation where the Word is preached.' By a right disposition, he meant hearing with discernment and humility. He added that 'we must labour to be affected with the word.' In other words, the word must shape our hopes, desires, fears and emotions. Finally, by duties practised afterwards, Perkins meant meditating on the sermon and applying it to our lives. 'The doctrine must be treasured up in our hearts, and practised in our lives.'[7]

Conclusion

Let's come back to the bacteria on your book. What would it take to ask them to get off? You could try saying, 'Please get off my book.' Presumably the sound waves would reach them.

But bacteria don't have ears. Can they even sense sound waves? And even if they could, what language do they speak? Even if you could find a common language, do they know what a book is? In so many ways the gulf between you and your bacteria is too big to bridge. It's a picture of the problem facing any attempt at communication between God and humanity.

And yet God in his greatness and grace does speak to us. In fact, he speaks in many different ways: in creation, in history, in the Bible, through preaching, and supremely through the person of his Son. People sometimes ask, 'If God exists, why doesn't he reveal himself more clearly?' But God is revealing himself all the time. The real question is, 'Will you listen?'

2

God spoke in the Bible

I sometimes co-write books with other people, and it's usually me who does the final edit. My ambition as I edit such books is to make it impossible for people to tell who wrote which chapter. I want the book to have a common feel so that readers are not distracted by changes of tone. But you couldn't claim that of the Bible. Obviously we expect poetry to feel different from history. But it's not just that it's made up of different types of literature. Mark's Gospel feels very different from John's Gospel. The personality of the writers shines through.

For example, you may have been taught at school not to start a sentence with the word 'And'. But turn to Mark 1 and, if you're reading from the NIV, you'll notice that verses 4, 7, 11, 13 and 34 all begin with the word 'And'. But that's nothing compared to the original Greek that Mark wrote. In Greek nearly every verse begins with 'and'. In fact, it's easier to list which verses *don't* begin with 'and' (verses 1–3, 8, 14, 24, 30, 32 and 45). Mark's also keen on the word 'immediately', which he uses in verses 10, 12, 18, 20, 21, 23, 29, 30 and 42 (ESV). It makes his prose breathless and relentless as he piles up the

evidence for the authority of Jesus ('And when . . . immediately . . . And . . . immediately . . . And . . .'). It's all action.

When you turn to John's Gospel, the feel is very different.
Much of the Gospel involves people talking to Jesus, with not
a lot going on. Interestingly, the young John was a bit of a
hothead (Mark 3:17; Luke 9:49–55). But by the time he writes
his Gospel, the impulse for immediate action seems to have
been replaced by a more reflective temperament.

The Bible is a very human book. Think about the pain and
confusion expressed in the book of Lamentations. Compare
that to the joy of the psalms of thanksgiving. Jeremiah appears
at times to be suffering from depression. Meanwhile the book
of Proverbs is full of tongue-in-cheek humour.

But the Bible is also a divine book. It's *God's* word.

Look on the cover of your Bible and it almost certainly says,
'Holy Bible'. The phrase 'Holy Scriptures' is used in Romans
1:2 and 2 Timothy 3:15, meaning 'sacred' or even 'divine'. God
has sanctified the Bible. There are many ways in which the
Bible is like any other book. It's made up of words in sentences
and paragraphs. It makes sense through the same grammatical rules as any other book. It contains stories, poetry and
laws that follow the conventions of their genre. But there are
also important ways in which the Bible is *unlike* any other
book. Other books can reflect or contain God's word (if they
accurately summarize biblical truth). But only the Bible *is*
God's sacred word. Only the Scriptures are the infallible record
of his revelation.

The divine person who makes the Bible 'holy' is the *Holy
Spirit*. The prophets who spoke in the Old Testament did so
because the Spirit of God came upon them. But the Spirit was
not only at work when the prophets first spoke. The Spirit
also ensured that the record of their revelation was reported
accurately.

It's the same with the New Testament. We've already seen how we have access to God's revelation in Christ through the 'apostolic testimony'. But how can we trust their testimony? After all, it's easy for people to forget things. People often fill in the gaps in their knowledge and use their imagination. Or perhaps the first disciples exaggerated for effect.

In response, we need to remember that the apostles weren't the only eyewitnesses during the period in which the New Testament was being written. Plenty of people saw Jesus in action, and at least 500 saw him after his resurrection (1 Corinthians 15:6). If the apostles had made mistakes or started making things up, then there were people around who would have corrected them. Indeed, much of Jesus' ministry had been witnessed by his enemies. If the apostles had started spreading propaganda or spinning the story, then his enemies would have been quick to put the record straight. This was an oral culture in which people were used to remembering stories and passing on eyewitness testimony. So from a human perspective, we have good reason to trust the New Testament accounts.

But God goes a step further to ensure that the Bible is reliable. In John 16:13–14, Jesus makes this promise to his disciples.

> When he, the Spirit of truth, comes, he will guide you into all the truth. He will not speak on his own; he will speak only what he hears, and he will tell you what is yet to come. He will glorify me because it is from me that he will receive what he will make known to you.

This is not a promise that the Spirit will help you and me understand the truth. It was given to the first apostles on the night before Jesus died. These are the people whom Jesus has specially chosen to be eyewitnesses of his words and actions. Now he promises that the Spirit will enable them to present an accurate account and a true interpretation of his work.

We see this interplay between the Holy Spirit and human authors whenever the Bible talks about how it was written.

Mark 12:35–37

> While Jesus was teaching in the temple courts, he asked, 'Why do the teachers of the law say that the Messiah is the son of David? David himself, speaking by the Holy Spirit, declared:
>
>> "The Lord said to my Lord:
>> 'Sit at my right hand
>> until I put your enemies
>> under your feet.'"
>
> David himself calls him "Lord". How then can he be his son?'

We don't need to concern ourselves with the bigger point Jesus is making. Simply notice how he introduces this quote from Psalm 110: 'David himself, speaking by the Holy Spirit, declared . . .' David declares these words. There was a human author. But David was 'speaking by the Holy Spirit'.

1 Peter 1:10–11

> Concerning this salvation, the prophets, who spoke of the grace that was to come to you, searched intently and with the greatest care, trying to find out the time and circumstances to which the Spirit of Christ in them was pointing when he predicted the sufferings of the Messiah and the glories that would follow.

The prophets 'searched intently and with the greatest care'. There was, as it were, a human process of research and investigation. But at the same time 'the Spirit of Christ in them was pointing' to the suffering and glory of the Messiah.

2 Peter 1:20–21

> You must understand that no prophecy of Scripture came about by the prophet's own interpretation of things. For prophecy never had its origin in the human will, but prophets, though human, spoke from God as they were carried along by the Holy Spirit.

The Spirit ensured that the writers of the Bible not only *recorded* what they saw and heard accurately, but also that they *interpreted* it accurately. The Bible is an annotated account of God's revelation in history. It provides its own explanation of the story it tells. Here Peter tells us that this explanation is divinely inspired. It was written down by human authors, and there's no doubt that they were human authors. But it didn't originate with those authors. They didn't make it up. They received it from God. They speak, but they speak from God. The words they say are words from God. They are the word *of* God.

2 Timothy 3:16–17

> All Scripture is God-breathed and is useful for teaching, rebuking, correcting and training in righteousness, so that the servant of God may be thoroughly equipped for every good work.

Some translations say, 'All Scripture is inspired.' But this isn't quite strong enough. You might say Beethoven was inspired when he wrote his Ninth Symphony or that a particular biography is an inspiring book. But Paul is saying more than this about the Bible. 'Spirit' and 'breath' are the same word in Greek. So 'God-breathed' is 'God-Spirited' or 'Spirited out by God'. If I speak to you, then my words come out of my body on my breath. In a similar way, the words of God come through the breath of God. So it's not that God inspired the human authors who then went away and wrote the Bible. The words came out from God through his Spirit. So when we speak of the 'inspiration' of the Bible, we mean something quite specific: the fact that it's God-breathed.[1]

Different authors wrote different books over a period of centuries in different cultures and at different times. The result ought to be a variety of competing perspectives. But instead, the Bible tells one big central story – the story of salvation in Jesus. How is that possible? Because the Spirit of truth was speaking through each author. So the Bible manages to speak both with many voices and with one voice. The work of the Spirit does not eradicate the personality of the different authors. Yet at the same time the work of the Spirit unifies their message.

How does this work? Evangelical Christians believe in 'plenary', 'verbal' and 'confluent' inspiration. We'd better find out what those words mean.

1. Plenary – everything you read

Our modern world is the product of the Enlightenment – the movement of thought in seventeenth- and eighteenth-century Europe which emphasized human reason. Enlightenment thinkers focused on the human side of the creation of Scripture. Some tried to identify the background sources that might have been used to compile the Bible in the form in which we have it today. Baruch Spinoza (1632–77), for example, questioned whether Moses was the author of the first five books of the Bible.

Exploring the possible sources in this way was not in itself a problem (although it has not generally proved a very useful exercise). The problem was that bigger things were going on. Enlightenment thinkers were emphasizing the human author to the exclusion of the divine author. So Spinoza also questioned the inspiration of the Scriptures. The prophets were inspired when they said, 'Thus says the Lord.' But the ordinary speech of the apostles or the historical accounts, he said, were not inspired. He pointed to the way Paul used arguments rather than simply made divine pronouncements.

In response to Spinoza, orthodox Christians affirmed *plenary inspiration*. The word 'plenary' means 'entire' or 'complete'. Paul said, '*All* Scripture is God-breathed.' In other words, plenary inspiration is a way of saying that it's not just the direct speech of prophets that is inspired. Everything you read in the Bible is divinely inspired.

Some people accept Jesus, but refuse to accept the authority of the whole Bible. They use the words of Jesus to judge which bits of the Bible they'll accept. But this isn't how *Jesus himself* treats the Bible. Let's take one example. In Matthew 19:4–5, Jesus quotes from Genesis 2:24: 'For this reason a man will leave his father and mother and be united to his wife, and the two will become one flesh.' These are not words spoken directly by God. They're an editorial comment on the story. Yet Jesus introduces them by saying, 'Haven't you read . . . that at the beginning the Creator "made them male and female," and said . . .' Jesus identifies the editorial comment of the human author as the words of the Creator. And he equates the words we 'read' with words spoken by God. If we take seriously the words of Jesus recorded in the

Gospels, then we need to take seriously the rest of the Bible as well!

Plenary or total inspiration doesn't mean all Scripture is equally relevant or important. No-one is suggesting you should write out 2 Timothy 4:13 and stick on your fridge: 'When you come, bring the cloak that I left with Carpus at Troas.' But even verses like this are inspired by God. And they might have some lessons for us on the frailty of Christian leaders and the need to care for one another.

2. Verbal – every word counts

In response to Spinoza, a Dutch theologian called Jean Leclerc said that the words were not inspired, but the doctrines were. This got round the 'ordinary speech' of the apostles that Spinoza had highlighted, along with other similar 'problems' like grammatical errors and differing descriptions of the same event.

More recently, Karl Barth has spoken of the Bible as a witness to revelation. Barth was perhaps the greatest theologian of the twentieth century and a fierce opponent of liberal theology. But his view of the Bible is deficient. According to Barth, the Bible is the window through which we see God's revelation in Jesus. In this analogy, the window may be dirty (Scripture may contain errors), but it still gives us a genuine view of what's beyond (Scripture still reveals Christ). This is the view of the Bible I was taught in my first year at university.

At first sight, this approach appears to offer a way round some of the apparent contradictions, while retaining a commitment to divine revelation. But there are two problems with this view. First, it's hard to know where to stop. When does revelation end and error begin? In the end we're left uncertain about the truth.

Second, this is not how the Bible describes itself. As we've seen, Paul says, 'All Scripture is God-breathed.' And that means individual words as well as big ideas. Quoting Deuteronomy, Jesus said, 'Man shall not live on bread alone, but on *every* word that comes from the mouth of God' (Matthew 4:4). Every word of the Bible comes from God.

So in response to people like Leclerc, evangelicals have affirmed *verbal inspiration*. The adjective 'verbal' means 'to do with words'. So verbal inspiration affirms that the words themselves are inspired – not just the thoughts.

3. Confluent – every author matters

Muslims believe that the Qur'an was dictated to the Prophet Mohammad. Mohammad played no part in its creation other than to write down what he was told. And many opponents of the inspiration of the Bible assumed it involved a similar process of dictation. And if the Bible was dictated, then it's hard to account for those parts that clearly reflect the personality of the human authors.

But this is not what Christians believe about the Bible. In a few cases there was dictation. Moses, for example, is told to write down what God has told him (Exodus 34:27). But at other times the human authors wrote down their own thoughts or drew on their own existing knowledge. Nevertheless, God so worked in them that their thoughts were God's thoughts. Luke, for example, was not sitting in quiet contemplation until the Spirit came upon him. He was busy researching his sources (Luke 1:1–4). Paul was not hanging around for the Spirit to give him an inspirational thought. He was writing letters off in a hurry to address some crisis or other that had blown up in one of the churches. They spoke, says Peter, 'as they were carried along by the Holy Spirit' (2 Peter 1:20–21).

The critique of divine inspiration is based on a false choice. It assumes either that God wrote the Bible, in which case the human authors were mere scribes, or that people wrote the Bible, in which case God did not write it. Since the Bible is clearly written by people, the assumption is that God was at best indirectly involved. J. I. Packer says of this argument,

> It assumes that God and man stand in such a relation to each other that they cannot both be free agents in the same action . . . But the Bible teaches rather that the freedom of God, who works in and through His creatures, leading them to act according to their nature, is itself the foundation and guarantee of the freedom of their action.[2]

There was a fusing of the human and divine elements. That's why we speak of *confluent inspiration*. The word 'confluent' means 'flowing together'. In geography a 'confluence' is a place where two rivers meet. In the Bible the 'rivers' of human and divine authorship meet together. Both the divine and human authors matter.

So in response to the Enlightenment, evangelicals developed the doctrine of the plenary, verbal, confluent inspiration of the Bible.

It is sometimes suggested that this is a new doctrine – and maybe even an evangelical obsession not shared by previous generations of Christians. But in fact the Church Fathers and Reformers unanimously affirmed Scripture to be divinely authored.[3] It may not have been developed as a doctrine, but this was because it was everywhere assumed. It wasn't affirmed in early creeds because no-one disputed it. So the doctrine of verbal inspiration is recent in *form*, because it was attacked in the Enlightenment. But the early Church Fathers introduced quotations by saying, 'The Holy Spirit says . . .'

They used the picture of the human author as a musical instrument through which the Holy Spirit breathed. They spoke of the Bible being without error. In the fourth century AD Jerome talked of divine authorship extending to every word and syllable, while Augustine said the Bible was uniquely authoritative and completely without error.

The Qur'an is always recited in Arabic. But because God intends to communicate through the Bible, there was a recognition from the beginning that it would be translated. The New Testament writers sometimes quote from the Septuagint, the Greek translation of the Old Testament. Yet, even though these quotes are translations, the New Testament treats them as God's word. Translation inevitably involves some interpretative choices because languages don't map on to one another word for word. Even more literal translations can mislead because sometimes there are not exact matches for words, and grammar works differently in different languages. All Bible translations sit on a spectrum from more literal word-for-word translations like the English Standard Version (ESV) and the New American Standard Bible (NASB), to sense-for-sense translations like the New International Version (NIV) and the New Living Translation (NLT), using what's called 'dynamic equivalence', to paraphrases like *The Message*. So the Greek and Hebrew originals remain our touchstone. They are the text of Scripture that is without error. But we can trust translations like the NIV and ESV, and we can treat them as God's word to us.

Supreme authority

The Catholic Church claims tradition goes hand in hand with the Bible as God's revelation. As a result, the Church determines what the Bible means. Human tradition is supreme.

Modernity uses reason to evaluate the Bible, discarding those elements it finds distasteful or incredible. Human reason is supreme. People in our postmodern world judge everything against their feelings. 'This is who I feel I am' has become the criterion by which we decide what is true. Human experience is supreme.

The problem is not tradition, reason or experience per se. Tradition is valuable for we stand on the shoulders of giants. Reason matters – just think of all that humanity has invented and discovered. Experience clearly shapes our identity. The problem is the *human* component in human tradition, human reason and human experience. Our understanding is limited because we're finite creatures, and biased because we're sinful creatures. But revelation is from God. And that makes all the difference. This is what the Reformers meant by *sola Scriptura*, 'Scripture alone'. They didn't reject tradition, reason or experience. But when push comes to shove, Scripture alone is always supreme.

If the words of the Bible are the words of God, then they have the authority of God. And that means they must be obeyed. They're not merely religious opinions, wise advice or inspiring thoughts. They're divine declarations. And that means the measure of how biblical we are is not how much of the Bible we know, but how much of it we live. James warns against people who hear the word, but don't do it. They're like people who look at themselves in a mirror, notice that their hair is all over the place, but then do nothing about it (James 1:22–25). That's what we're like if we look into the Bible, see that our lives are not aligned to God's will and then do nothing about it. Sometimes people talk about the need to look for a Bible-teaching church. That's important. But what we really want to be is Bible-*doing* churches.

There's a Woody Allen comedy routine from the 1960s in which he describes getting kidnapped. The kidnappers send a ransom note to his parents. 'My father has bad reading habits,' says Allen. 'So he got into bed at night with the ransom note and he read half of it and got drowsy and fell asleep. Then he lent it out.' It's funny because it's so ridiculous. A ransom note is too important to neglect. Or imagine an envelope drops on to your mat with the Buckingham Palace logo on the front. I received a letter recently from my accountants and I didn't open it for a couple of days. But what if you received a letter from the Queen? You would hardly put it to one side to read later. You would be desperate to know what was inside.

If you really believe in the divine inspiration of the Holy Scripture, then you'll make reading the Bible and hearing it preached a top priority. That's because 'divine inspiration' means this is a message from God. It's the most important news from the most important person. And that's a message you're not going to postpone.

Enduring authority

The sociologist Zygmunt Bauman describes modern life as 'liquid'. Everything is fluid. Marriage, institutions, ideologies are all being emptied of content and authority. Along with this, words routinely exceed their meaning. Advertisers use big words to sell small things. Ghostwriting drains words of their authenticity. Politicians make promises or issue warnings in which their words exceed reality. So words are losing their value in our age. We suffer from what we might call 'word inflation'.

But the words of the Bible are 'enduring' and 'firm' because they're God's words (Psalm 19:9). The Word from which all the other words of God derive is Jesus, and Jesus is the eternal Word. The apostle Peter says,

> All people are like grass,
>> and all their glory is like the flowers of the field;
> the grass withers and the flowers fall,
>> but the word of the Lord endures for ever.
> (1 Peter 1:24–25)

He is quoting from Isaiah 40:6–8. Isaiah's words were already 800 years old when Peter quoted them. Now they're 2,800 years old. Compare this to what you read on social media. How much of that will be read in 2,800 years' time?

You can hold some very old things in your hands. The oldest thing I own is a Roman coin. It is nearly 2,000 years old – a piece of history from the days of the apostle Paul. But the Bible is a word from the eternal God and it endures throughout history. What else can you hold in your hands and say that about?

Other books can have a big impact on your life. And sometimes their impact is more immediate than the Bible. But that impact will fade. One day they'll be out of date. But the Bible is never out of date. It's important to have a sense of this. Why do we love Christian books? Why do we sometimes prefer to read them rather than the Bible? Perhaps because they offer a quick fix. They're like sugary cereals compared to 'porridge'. Sugar gives us a quick high, but soon leaves us feeling hungry again. If you want to develop as a person or acquire a new skill, then other books might produce more immediate effects. There's nothing wrong with that. But if you want to develop character that endures, then read the Book that endures. If you want to become a person of real substance, then read the Book of real substance. Let the enduring word of God shape who you are.

3

God speaks in the Bible

Hebrews 3:7 says, 'So, as the Holy Spirit says: "Today, if you hear his voice . . ."' The writer is introducing a quote from Psalm 95. Hebrews 4:7 introduces exactly the same quote with the words, 'God . . . spoke through David.' These are the words of both David and the Holy Spirit. That's the pattern we saw in the previous chapter.

As the Holy Spirit says

But look again at Hebrews 3:7. It doesn't just say, 'As the Holy Spirit *said*' – past tense. It says, 'As the Holy Spirit *says*' – present tense. Psalm 95 was already 1,000 years old when the letter of Hebrews was written. So these words had been written down a long time ago. Yet Hebrews uses the *present* tense. The Holy Spirit not only spoke when the words were first written; the Holy Spirit speaks every time they're read.

Consider the different ways the writer of Hebrews introduces quotes from the Old Testament:

1. *A human being spoke in the past through the Bible*
   'But there is a place where someone has testified . . .' (2:6).
   'As has just been said . . .' (3:15).
2. *God spoke in the past through the Bible*
   '. . . just as God has said . . .' (4:3).
   'God has said . . .' (13:5).
3. *Both God and a human being spoke in the past through the Bible*
   'God . . . spoke through David . . .' (4:7).
4. *The Father speaks in the present through the Bible*
   'Have you completely forgotten this word of encouragement that addresses you as a father addresses his son? . . . "My son . . ."' (12:5).
5. *Jesus speaks in the present through the Bible*
   'Jesus is not ashamed to call them brothers and sisters. He says . . . And again . . . And again he says . . .' (2:11–13).
6. *The Spirit speaks in the present through the Bible*
   'So, as the Holy Spirit says . . .' (3:7).
   'The Holy Spirit also testifies to us about this. First he says . . .' (10:15).
7. *We speak in the present through the Bible*
   'So we say with confidence . . .' (13:6).

In the first three examples, we see again that the Bible was written by both human beings and God. These verses all speak of this as an event in the past. But in examples 4–6, each member of the Trinity speaks today through the Bible. God the Father 'addresses' us (present tense) in the Bible – just as your father might talk to you (if your father is still alive). Jesus 'says' the words of Scripture (present tense) to affirm his solidarity with his people. And as we've seen in 3:7, the Spirit speaks (present tense) in and through the Bible.

In the final example, the Bible gives *us* words to say back to God. Here the divine and human come together in a remarkable way. God spoke through a human author in the past to give words to human beings to speak in the present to God. They are doubly human words – once when they were written, and again when they're spoken. Yet they're also divine words which begin and end with God. This is true of Hebrews 13:6, but it's also true of every psalm, hymn, creed and prayer in the Bible. The words of the Bible become divine–human words afresh when we speak them to God in prayer or praise.

The Spirit activates the Bible

Here's the key principle: the Spirit that worked in the hearts of the *writers* of the Bible to ensure what they *wrote* was God's word is the same Spirit that works in the hearts of *readers* of the Bible to ensure what we *hear* is God's word. The Spirit, as it were, activates the Bible as it's read or preached.

Genesis 1:2 says the wind of God or 'the Spirit of God was hovering over the waters'. The word of God by which he created the world came in the power of the Spirit. Psalm 33:6 says,

> By the word of the LORD the heavens were made,
>   their starry host by the breath of his mouth.

Remember 'breath' and 'Spirit' are the same word in Hebrew. Just as when I speak, my words travel from my mouth on my breath, so the Father's Word, Jesus, went forth on his breath, the Spirit, to accomplish his purposes. And his breath brought life. The first man was a mere lump of man-shaped clay until God breathed life into his soul (Genesis 2:7).

That pattern remains the same throughout the story of redemption. God's word goes forth in the power of the Spirit to bring life. Psalm 119:25 says,

My soul clings to the dust;
> give me life according to your word!

(ESV)

In Genesis, dust is a picture of lifelessness and death (Genesis 2:7; 3:19). So a soul clinging to dust is an image of a person who is so emotionally wrung out he feels close to death. But God breathes life into our souls through his Spirit-breathed word.

In Ezekiel 37 the prophet is shown a valley of dry bones which represent God's spiritually dead people. Ezekiel is told to prophecy to them: 'Dry bones, hear the word of the LORD!' (37:4). As a result, the bones come together, flesh appears and skin covers them. It's a demonstration of the power of God's word. But it is not enough, because the breath of the Spirit of God is not in the people. 'But there was no breath in them,' says verse 8. These bodies are lifeless forms. They're like the man-shaped clay in the garden of Eden. Ezekiel is faced with a valley of zombies. So God tells Ezekiel to 'prophesy to the breath'. 'So I prophesied as he commanded me,' says Ezekiel, 'and breath entered them; they came to life and stood up on their feet – a vast army' (37:10). It's only when God's word goes forth in the power of God's Spirit that it brings life, and God's Spirit operates as God's word is proclaimed.

The objective revelation of God is not enough, because our hearts are deaf to God's word. Left to ourselves, we block out the voice of God in our lives. We are predisposed by our sin to reject or twist or ignore God's revelation. We want to live our lives without God's 'interference' and we think we can manage without God's assistance. 'The person without the Spirit does not accept the things that come from the Spirit of God but considers them foolishness, and cannot understand them because they are discerned only through the Spirit' (1 Corinthians 2:14).

But God in his love gives the Spirit so we receive his word *as* his word. The Spirit opens our eyes to see the glory of Christ. Then the Bible stops being bad news of divine interference and becomes good news of divine grace.

> For who knows a person's thoughts except their own spirit within them? In the same way no one knows the thoughts of God except the Spirit of God. What we have received is not the spirit of the world, but the Spirit who is from God, so that we may understand what God has freely given us.
> (1 Corinthians 2:11–12)

The word of God comes alive as we read it through the life-giving Spirit. We've already talked about those times when we read the Bible or hear it preached and find ourselves exposed by the word or hear it speaking with uncanny precision. But those moments are signs of what happens *every* time the Bible is read.

The Bible is a busy book

This present-tense-ness of the Bible means it's never a dead letter. Hebrews 4:12 says that 'the word of God is alive and active'. It's almost as if you could put it to your ear and hear it pulsing! It's a dynamic process. It's not just that we learn a few extra facts. The living God speaks to us through his word.

It's really important that the Bible is a historical account of historical events. If we don't see it like this, then our faith rests on feelings and experiences. And feelings and experiences can come and go. It's a shaky foundation. Christianity is rooted in historical events when God acted to save a people for himself. Indeed, God identifies himself through his historical acts. So historical facts matters to us. Without the fact of the resurrection our faith is futile, says Paul in 1 Corinthians 15:17. So the Bible is never less than a historical record.

But the Bible is also *more than* an account of what God has done and said in the past. God is at work through the Bible. He is doing things *now in the present* through his word. So the Bible doesn't simply record the story of salvation; it's also part of that story. God uses the Bible to awaken cold hearts and open blind eyes. We're saved by believing in the gospel, and the Bible conveys the gospel to us. So, for example, in 1 Corinthians 1:18 Paul doesn't simply say that the cross is the power of God. He says that '*the message* of the cross . . . is the power of God'. If Christ had simply died and risen, how could we put our faith in him? The Bible and Christ go together. We're saved by Christ alone. But we encounter Christ in the Bible. The two are linked: Christ is the incarnate Word, and the Bible is the written word.

Imagine an amazing offer in one of your local shops. All the books Tim Chester has ever written are on sale for 1p. What a bargain! But no-one knows about it. There's no advertising. No signs. As a result, no-one takes advantage of the offer. Now imagine that it's eternal life on offer, and its price tag says, 'Free'. The price has already been paid. All you need to do is ask. But no-one knows about it. No-one would receive the gift of salvation because no-one would know about it. Salvation only works if God also reveals the gospel in the Bible and puts it to work through the Holy Spirit.

So the Bible is an integral part of God's plan of salvation. The Bible – read, preached, chatted or summarized – is what

God uses to awaken faith in the hearts of unbelievers and strengthen the faith of believers.

The Bible is a busy book. It's always at work.

In John 14:10 Jesus says, 'The words I say to you I do not speak on my own authority. Rather, it is the Father, living in me, who . . .' How would you expect Jesus to finish this sentence? I anticipate him saying, 'speaking through me' or 'speaking his words'. But in fact Jesus says that the Father 'is *doing his work*'. When repairs are being made to the road, the workers involved put up a men-at-work sign to warn motorists. Our Bibles need a God-at-work sign on the front.

At creation God created through his word. Into the darkness and chaos, 'God said, "Let there be light," and there was light' (Genesis 1:3). God simply spoke a word and the world came into being in all its beauty and complexity. After the fall God begins the re-establishment of his rule through a word: the covenant word of promise that he speaks to Abraham. And that pattern continues throughout the story of the Bible. God rules through his word and restores his rule through his word. He saves through his word and renews through his word. In 2 Corinthians 4:5–6 Paul says,

> For what we preach is not ourselves, but Jesus Christ as Lord, and ourselves as your servants for Jesus' sake. For God, who said, 'Let light shine out of darkness,' made his light shine in our hearts to give us the light of the knowledge of God's glory displayed in the face of Christ.

Just as God created through his word, so now he *recreates* through his word. The divine word that brought life to the world is the same divine word that brings new life to dead hearts.

Not only does God work through his word, he *always* works through his word. The living word is alive and at work even when it is rejected. Paul says,

> We are to God the pleasing aroma of Christ among those who are being saved and those who are perishing. To the one we are an aroma that brings death; to the other, an aroma that brings life. And who is equal to such a task? Unlike so many, we do not peddle the word of God for profit. On the contrary, in Christ we speak before God with sincerity, as those sent from God.
>
> (2 Corinthians 2:15–17)

When we share God's word, people respond in contrasting ways: with acceptance or rejection. But either way, God's word is at work. It's a sobering thought. If people receive those words (a process that may take some time), then those words are life-giving. But if people reject our message, then those words harden them in their rebellion and confirm their judgment.

In 1903 Barclay Buxton, together with his co-worker Paget Wilkes, launched the Japan Evangelistic Band at the Keswick Convention. In 1942 a missionary called Mary Sander wrote to Barclay Buxton with whom she had served in Japan:

> I feel, on looking back, that the way God used me to win Japanese to Christ was in the way you taught us in the use of the Scriptures, His own Word, the weapon of the Word, and His Spirit. It did the work. I remember feeling what comfort it was that not our weak words, but His eternal Word was the weapon of our warfare. It seemed like a strong friend at hand.[1]

A contemporary word

It's easy for us to think of the Bible as an old book. In one sense that's obviously true. The early parts of it were written over 3,000 years ago. But that doesn't mean the Bible is out of date. Indeed, in some ways it's ever new, always speaking with new relevance to each new generation. So the New Testament writers spoke of the Old Testament Scriptures as written 'for us', even though the readers of the New Testament weren't the original intended audience:

> But about the resurrection of the dead – have you not read what God said *to you*, 'I am the God of Abraham, the God of Isaac, and the God of Jacob'?
> (Matthew 22:31–32)

> [Moses] was in the assembly in the wilderness, with the angel who spoke to him on Mount Sinai, and with our ancestors; and he received *living words to pass on to us*.
> (Acts 7:38)

> For everything that was written in the past was *written to teach us*, so that through the endurance taught in the Scriptures and the encouragement they provide we might have hope.
> (Romans 15:4)

> These things happened to them as examples and were *written down as warnings for us*, on whom the culmination of the ages has come.
> (1 Corinthians 10:11)

If we think of the Bible as an old book, then we'll assume it's our job to make it relevant. We'll think we need to take a message belonging to another age and translate it to our age. We'll try to pick out the enduring principles, brush off the dust of the ages and then rework them for our day.

Sometimes people ask for what they call 'practical' preaching. They want to know how to be better parents or more successful workers. There's not necessarily anything wrong with this if the answers connect us to the central plotline of the Bible. The Bible does speak to the issues of the modern world. But sometimes what is offered is the latest pop psychology or management speak dressed up with a few proof-texts. All we hear is an echo of the world around us. It might feel relevant, but it doesn't really equip us to face the ups and downs of life. It all too easily becomes a legalistic 'six steps' to a better life. It's not the gospel and so it's not good news.

But it's also unnecessary. We don't need to 'apply' the Bible if by that we mean take the truth and transfer it over to our world. Don't get me wrong. Nothing is more important than putting the Bible into practice – it is, as we've seen, the word of God. But the point I'm making is this: we don't need to 'make' the Bible relevant because it's *already* relevant. Our job is merely to *show* how it's relevant and follow the connections that are already there. The Bible is a contemporary word.

One reason why it's always contemporary is that the fundamental truths about life, the world and people don't change. It's true we have mobile phones, longer lives, liberal democracies; so in many ways our lives are very different from our forebears. But we're still people made in God's image. We're still made to know God and find our identity in him. We're still rebels against his rule who face his judgment. We still long for the world to be made new. We're still in need of a Saviour. And Jesus is still the only Saviour of humanity.

The Bible speaks to all these issues like no other book. It still contains the true, ultimate and only hope for the world. Writing to the church in Ephesus in the first century, the risen Christ says, 'Whoever has ears, let them hear what the Spirit says to the churches' (Revelation 2:7). Although his words are addressed to one particular church at one particular time, we're to hear what the Spirit says (present tense again) to all the churches (plural).

The other reason why the Bible is always contemporary is that it's a *living* word. It never grows old and it never dies. It lives because it's enlivened by the Spirit of life!

You may think I'm being a bit picky. But this matters. If we try to 'make' the Bible relevant, we open ourselves up to two dangers. First, we might misapply it. We make the Bible say something contemporary. But when you 'make' the Bible say something, the chances are you're communicating your thoughts rather than God's thoughts.

The second danger is even more significant. If we think the Bible isn't a contemporary word, then we'll be tempted to update it. We'll select from the Bible or reinterpret it to make it fit our culture. The issue of sexuality is a current example of this. What the Bible says is out of step with our culture. As a result, the Bible feels old-fashioned. If we think our job is to make it relevant, then our tendency will be to reinterpret it so it fits better in our world. We might talk about 'trajectories' that lead to an acceptance of gay practice, or emphasize love over truth. In the end you make the Bible say the opposite of what it actually says. But if we start by assuming that the Bible is a contemporary word, then we discover its teaching on sexuality has never been more relevant. Instead of confirming our current culture, it challenges it head-on. We're to make our assumptions fit with the Bible, and not the other way round.

Listen for God's voice

We've seen that God speaks in the Bible through his Spirit. This means you may need to change your attitude to reading the Bible. You may have read it to tick a passage off your list, or out of intellectual curiosity, or to impress others with your Bible quotes, or to learn more information about God. God is inviting you to listen for his voice.

So read the Bible with expectation. Look at what God's word does in Psalm 19:7–13:

> The law of the LORD is perfect,
>   refreshing the soul.
> The statutes of the LORD are trustworthy,
>   making wise the simple.
> The precepts of the LORD are right,
>   giving joy to the heart.
> The commands of the LORD are radiant,
>   giving light to the eyes.
> The fear of the LORD is pure,
>   enduring for ever.
> The decrees of the LORD are firm
>   and all of them are righteous.
> They are more precious than gold,
>   than much pure gold;
> they are sweeter than honey,
>   than honey from the honeycomb.
> By them your is servant warned;
>   in keeping them there is great reward.
> Who can discern their own errors?
>   Forgive my hidden faults.
> Keep your servant also from wilful sins;
>   may they not rule over me.

Then will I be blameless,
  innocent of great transgression.

Expect God to speak to you so that he refreshes your soul, makes you wise, gives joy to your heart, gives light to your eyes, warns you of sin, exposes your heart, sets you free and leads you to your reward in Christ.

Pray before you read, asking God to speak to you. There are many ways of articulating this. As you read, pray that the Holy Spirit would refresh your soul, make you wise, give joy to your heart and light to your eyes. Ask the Spirit to expose your sin and set you free from its power by redirecting your desires to your true reward in Christ. Above all, pray that the Spirit would reveal the glory of God in the face of Jesus Christ. Psalm 119 is full of prayers you can pray as you come to God's word. How about Psalm 119:18: 'Open my eyes that I may see wonderful things in your law'? Or Psalm 119:28: 'My soul is weary with sorrow; strengthen me according to your word'?

I realize that time often feels short. Here's my experience. If my attitude as I read God's word is, 'I've got to get through this quickly so I can get on with my day', it's usually a fairly empty process. But if my concern is to hear God's voice and meet him in his word, then it becomes much more significant. I've noticed that often this doesn't take much longer. It's much more about my attitude than my schedule.

But it is also a question of priorities. People who spend more time with God in his word don't have more hours in the day. They simply have different priorities. We always make time for what we think is important. And what's more important than hearing God's voice?

A tree by a stream

Psalm 1 begins:

> Blessed is the one
> who does not walk in step with the wicked
> or stand in the way that sinners take
> or sit in the company of mockers,
> but whose delight is in the law of the LORD,
> and who meditates on his law day and night.
> That person is like a tree planted by streams of water,
> which yields its fruit in season
> and whose leaf does not wither –
> whatever they do prospers.

If we meditate on God's word, then we'll be like 'a tree planted by streams of water'. There are plenty of kooky and unhelpful approaches to meditation in the world around us that can give meditation a bad name. But meditation is a big deal in the Bible. Christian meditation always involves reflecting on God's revelation. That could be his revelation in creation or his providence in our lives. But primarily its focus is God's word, read and preached. It always involves understanding the passage. We're not looking for meaning in addition to the message intended by the author. We're exploring the implications of the author's message for our hearts and our lives. The aim is to understand the passage with our *heads*, be captivated by it in our *hearts* and turn it into action with our *hands*.

At its simplest, meditation simply means thinking about a passage – turning it over in your mind and in your imagination. You can do it in your armchair in the morning as you read the Bible. You can do it while you're driving to work or pumping iron in the gym. William Tyndale urged his readers to 'think that every syllable pertaineth to thine own self, and suck out the pith of the scriptures'.[2]

Have a go at placing yourself in the passage. How might you have reacted if you'd been there? Or think of meditation as preaching to yourself. How does the word speak to you? What do you receive from Christ? What does it say about your identity in Christ? What's the response to which it calls you? What motives does it give?

Consider David's approach to God's word in Psalm 119:

> I have hidden your word in my heart
>   that I might not sin against you.
> (verse 11)

> I delight in your decrees;
>   I will not neglect your word.
> (verse 16)

> Your decrees are the theme of my song
> (verse 54)

> Oh, how I love your law!
>   I meditate on it all day long.
> (verse 97)

> I stand in awe of your laws.
> (verse 120)

> I open my mouth and pant,
>   longing for your commands.
> (verse 131)

> My heart trembles at your word.
> (verse 161)

Hide God's word in your heart. Sing God's word. Tremble before it. Stand in awe at what it says. Or open your mouth and pant for it, gulping it down like someone out of breath.

Don't miss the focus on the heart. The blessed person is the one 'whose *delight* is in the law of the LORD'. Let the passage capture your imagination. Let it lead you to your Saviour's feet. Look for the glory of God in the face of Jesus Christ. Listen to the voice of God who still speaks through his word.

Notice too that Psalm 1 doesn't begin with meditation. First, we need to screen out other voices. The wicked, sinners and mockers of verse 1 represent the voice of our culture – what the New Testament calls 'the world' (1 John 2:15–17). This clearly involves avoiding influences that directly cause us to doubt God's word or lead us into temptation. But we also need to make room for God's word. We live in a noisy world. We have the radio on in the car. We walk round wearing headphones. We watch the television while catching up with social media on our smartphones. There's no room for God's word to take root, no space for the prompting of the Spirit, no time to reflect. And when we do try to meditate, a hundred other things swirl round our minds. All because we suffer from 'fomo' – the 'fear of missing out'. And as a result, we miss out on the blessing God promises to those who meditate on his word. So go for a walk without your phone. Read your Bible away from your computer. Turn the radio off when you're doing the chores. Build space to think into your life. Don't be afraid of silence or boredom – use these moments to meditate and pray. We fill our lives with distractions and then wonder why we can't hear God's voice.

4

God speaks Jesus in the Bible

Two men were once walking along a road, their faces downcast, talking in sombre tones. Gradually, a third man caught up and fell in step with them. He asked what they were talking about. They stopped. This news was far too weighty to be shared while walking. Indeed, they were astonished that the stranger hadn't heard about it already. How could anyone have missed the momentous events that had just taken place? They explained how Jesus of Nazareth, the man they hoped would redeem Israel, had been executed by the Romans. 'We had hoped,' they said. But now all hope was gone. Moreover, weird stories were circulating: his body was gone and someone had seen an angel.

Then it was the stranger's turn to speak. His words must have come as a shock: 'How foolish you are.' The day was the first Easter Sunday, the place was the road to Emmaus and the stranger was Jesus himself, freshly risen from the grave.

The words of Jesus to the two disciples are perhaps something of a surprise. We might have expected him to say, 'Here I am. I've risen from the dead.' But instead he does a Bible study:

> He said to them, 'How foolish you are, and how slow
> to believe all that the prophets have spoken! Did not the
> Messiah have to suffer these things and then enter his glory?'
> And beginning with Moses and all the Prophets, he explained
> to them what was said in all the Scriptures concerning
> himself.
> (Luke 24:25–27)

Jesus says 'all the Scriptures' are about him. 'Moses and all the Prophets' was one way first-century Jews referred to what we call the Old Testament – the Bible in the form in which it existed at that point (before the New Testament was written). So Jesus is saying that the Bible is all about the suffering and glory of the Messiah. Peter echoes this language when he says that the prophets spoke of 'the sufferings of the Messiah and the glories that would follow' (1 Peter 1:10–11). Not only that, but the disciples should have realized this. Indeed, Jesus implies they were a bit stupid to have missed the point of the Bible so badly. His death and resurrection shouldn't have taken them by surprise. Jesus says the same thing later on the same day when he appears to more of his disciples:

> He said to them, 'This is what I told you while I was still
> with you: everything must be fulfilled that is written about
> me in the Law of Moses, the Prophets and the Psalms.'
>   Then he opened their minds so they could understand
> the Scriptures. He told them, 'This is what is written: the
> Messiah will suffer and rise from the dead on the third
> day, and repentance for the forgiveness of sins will be
> preached in his name to all nations, beginning at
> Jerusalem.'
> (Luke 24:44–47)

Again, Jesus is saying the *whole* of the Old Testament is about the death and resurrection of the Messiah, and the mission to the nations. In John 5:39–40 Jesus had said to the Jewish leaders, 'You study the Scriptures diligently because you think that in them you have eternal life. These are the very Scriptures that testify about me, yet you refuse to come to me to have life.' And there are many other occasions when Jesus identifies himself as the fulfilment of specific Scriptures (Matthew 13:13–14; 26:53–54; Mark 9:11–13; 11:15–17; 14:27; Luke 4:16–21; 22:37; John 13:18).

It's no surprise to hear that the Bible is about Jesus. After all, it contains the four Gospels that tell the story of his life. Jesus is also the big theme of the preaching in Acts and he's clearly central to the teaching of the New Testament letters. And there are some famous prophecies in the Old Testament about his coming. Every Christmas we read, 'For to us a child is born, to us a son is given' (Isaiah 9:6).

But Jesus is making a much bigger claim. He's saying *all* the Scriptures are about him. The Old Testament consistently and relentlessly looks forward to his coming. Then the New Testament describes and explains his coming as well as looking ahead to his return. Everywhere we look, we're meant to see Jesus.

The Father speaks in the Bible, and Jesus is the Word that he speaks. Red-letter Bibles print the direct words of Jesus in red so they stand out to give them special status. The irony is that this is self-defeating, for red text is less legible than black text, so the effect is actually to make the direct words of Jesus *less* significant! More importantly, it assumes that the rest of the Bible is not the words of Jesus. But Jesus is the Word of God. All revelation is in him and through him. All the words in the Bible are the words of Jesus about Jesus.

Understanding the punchline

The Bible is one story in two halves: the Old and New Testaments. And like any story, half the story on its own doesn't really make sense. The Old Testament without the New Testament is like a joke without a punchline. And the New Testament without the Old Testament is like a punchline without the build-up. We need to read the Old Testament as Jesus read it – as a witness to him and his work. We need to read it as Christians. The early Church Father Irenaeus said, 'If anyone, therefore, reads the Scriptures with attention, he will find in them an account of Christ . . . The treasure hid in the Scriptures is Christ.'[1]

How does this work? Any individual Bible story is part of the wider story of redemption, the story of how God fulfils his purposes for his people. All the stories of the Old Testament are in fact part of this one story, the story that begins with creation and finishes with the new creation. The recognition that we ourselves are part of the same story as the Old Testament is an important step along the way to recognizing its significance for us today. The history of the people of God in the Old Testament is our history. Their story is our story.

So we fail to understand the Old Testament if we see it as illustrating eternal truths or make it a collection of morality tales. In fact, if we do this, then we end up preaching legalism. We simply tell people how they should live, without offering the goodness of grace in Christ. But viewing all the Bible from the perspective of Christ enables us to see the grace of God everywhere.

Here are four questions that may help. When reading any passage of Scripture, especially Old Testament passages, ask yourself:

- What aspects of the character of God does the passage reveal and how does Christ exemplify these?
- What aspects of the identity of humanity does the passage reveal and how does Christ fulfil these?
- What aspects of the promises of God does the passage reveal and how does Christ complete these?
- What aspects of the need of humanity does the passage reveal and how does Christ meet these?

What ties together the stories of the Bible and links them to Christ are the promises of God to Adam, Abraham, Moses and David. The Bible is the story of how God fulfils and expands those promises. So viewing the Old Testament passages as fulfilled in Christ means viewing them in the light of the history of promise. The primary way we're to read each individual story is in the context of the story of God's unfolding promises.

Genesis 1 – 3 describes how God made a good world and made humanity to enjoy his world. He placed us under his good rule – a rule that brought life and freedom. But humanity rejected God's rule and incurred God's wrath. The rest of the Bible is the story of how God sets about restoring what was lost and fulfilling his purposes in creation.

God's promise to Adam is given indirectly through the cursing of the serpent:

> I will put enmity
>   between you and the woman,
>   and between your offspring and hers;
> he will crush your head,
>   and you will strike his heel.
> (Genesis 3:15)

Here's the promise of a coming Saviour who will defeat Satan and undo his destructive work. Both humanity and the earth have been cursed as a result of our rebellion. But the Serpent-Crusher will restore humanity and renew creation.

This promise comes into sharper focus with the promise to Abraham. God promises Abraham a people and a land. He also promises to bless all nations through Abraham. These are the promises that drive the story of the exodus. The covenant with Moses then enshrines them in the identity of God's people, Israel.

The covenant with David adds the promise of a king. It was implicit because Abraham was promised a kingdom (Genesis 17:6), and the practice of kingship was regulated in the law of Moses (Deuteronomy 17). But with David, the promise of an everlasting kingdom ruled over by God's king becomes explicit. As the kings of Israel fail to lead the people faithfully, the expectation grows of a coming Saviour-King, the Messiah from the line of David, who would rescue God's people.

There are then four elements to the promise of God:[2]

1. *A people who know God*
   I will make you into a great nation,
      and I will bless you;
   I will make your name great,
      and you will be a blessing.
   (Genesis 12:2)
2. *A place of rest*
   'The LORD appeared to Abram and said, "To your offspring I will give this land"' (Genesis 12:7).
3. *Blessing to the nations*
   I will bless those who bless you,
      and whoever curses you I will curse;

and all peoples on earth
> will be blessed through you.
(Genesis 12:3)
4. *A king and a kingdom*
'I will establish the throne of his kingdom for ever. I will be his father, and he shall be my son' (2 Samuel 7:13–14).

The Old Testament is the story of how God partially fulfils these promises in the life of Israel. But each partial fulfilment points to its ultimate fulfilment through Jesus.

This allows us to see how any particular story fits in the story of God's promise. As we read the Old Testament, we can see how God is partially fulfilling each strand of his promises in the story of Israel:

- The partial *fulfilments* of the promise illustrate the ultimate fulfilment in Christ.
- The *partial* nature of their fulfilment points to the need for Christ to fulfil God's promises fully.

And along the way the promise gets bigger. When God comes to Abraham, the promise focuses on one family and one patch of land. But as the story unfolds, it becomes clear that only a renewed humanity in a renewed world will fulfil God's ultimate purposes.

So as you read an Old Testament story, ask yourself:

- What is happening to each element of the promise at this point in the story?
- What does this story tell us about God and his rule?
- How does it contrast with, point to or illuminate the work of Christ?

- How does it give us confidence in the word of promise that comes to us in the gospel?
- What does it tell us about how people are to respond to the word of promise?

After they journey with Jesus on the road to Emmaus, those two disciples said, 'Were not our hearts burning within us while he talked with us on the road and opened the Scriptures to us?' (Luke 24:32). If you want your heart to be set on fire, then look for Jesus in the whole Bible.

The Bible is good news

Because the central message of the Bible is Jesus, it's good news. Consider how Paul opens the letter of Romans:

> Paul, a servant of Christ Jesus, called to be an apostle and set apart for the gospel of God – the gospel he promised beforehand through his prophets in the Holy Scriptures regarding his Son . . . (Romans 1:1–3)

Notice how the gospel, the Scriptures and Jesus are all closely connected. The gospel is about Jesus and the gospel is promised in the Scriptures.

What is the gospel? The word means 'good news', and the gospel is the good news of Jesus – his life, death, resurrection, ascension and return to judge sinners and renew all things, along with the promise of forgiveness, justification and adoption to all who entrust themselves to him. So the gospel is a summary of the Bible's central message. It can be stated in just three words: 'Jesus is Lord' (Romans 10:9), or a line like 'Christ Jesus came into the world to save sinners' (1 Timothy 1:15). That's the gospel in super-summary form.

It could be a larger summary: a sermon or talk, a book (like *Basic Christianity* by John Stott)[3] or a course (like Christianity Explored).[4] But whether it's a three-word summary, a conversation over a cup of tea, a thirty-minute sermon or the whole Bible, the gospel is the word of God.

So the gospel is not the same thing as the Bible, but neither is it entirely different. The authoritative source for the gospel message is the Bible. Paul says that 'the gospel' was 'promised beforehand through his prophets in the Holy Scriptures' (Romans 1:2). He says, 'Scripture foresaw that God would justify the Gentiles by faith, and announced the gospel in advance to Abraham: "All nations will be blessed through you"' (Galatians 3:8).

The laws and warnings of Scripture must be seen in the light of its overall movement towards redemption in Christ. There are laws and warnings in the Bible, but they're not an alternative or a supplement to the gospel. The Bible is not like a too-good-to-be-true offer with the law as the nasty surprise hidden in the small print. We don't sign people up using the gospel and then hit them with the law. The law in the Old Testament was designed to reveal our need of a Saviour and illuminate the work of our Saviour. The commands of Scripture flow from the new identity we have in Christ, a truth to which we'll return in chapter 9.

The Bible is a missional book[5]

The Bible is missional because mission is central to the plotline of the Bible:

- God promises Abraham a people. And the Bible is the story of how God redeems his people and gathers them through the proclamation of his word.

- God promises a place of blessing. And the Bible is the story of how God will renew creation in Christ and how he is bringing his exiled people home through the mission of the church.
- God promises Abraham that his family will be a blessing to all nations. And the Bible is the story of how God blesses the nations through the coming of his Son and the witness of his people as they model the blessing of living under God's rule.
- God promises a king and a kingdom. And the Bible is the story of how God re-establishes his rule through King Jesus and how that rule is extended through the proclamation of the gospel as we invite people to submit to Christ and experience his rule as joy, freedom, peace and life.

The Bible is missional because so much of it is written from mission or for mission. Jonah's story is a prophetic call to Israel to have compassion on the nations. John's Gospel is an evangelistic book written to encourage people to believe in Jesus (John 20:31). Paul's letters were written to new church plants as they wrestled with the challenges of growth. Romans is written to show how Paul's mission to the Gentiles arises out of the plot of the Old Testament and to recruit support for his mission to Spain.

The Bible is missional because the Bible is the means and mark of mission. The book of Acts is peppered with summary statements about the word of God spreading (Acts 2:41–47; 6:7; 9:31; 12:24; 16:5; 19:20). Acts 6:7, for example, says, 'So the word of God spread.' Spreading the word was the *means* by which the church grew, and the spread of the word was the *mark* of its growth.

Above all, the Bible is missional because it's all about Jesus and therefore it's good news. And news is something you pass on.

Let's come back to the two disciples who walked with Jesus along the Emmaus road. Jesus showed them how he was the focus of the Bible. As a result, the strangest thing happened: 'They got up and returned at once to Jerusalem' (Luke 24:33). Think how significant this is. They do what they had urged Christ not to do – they take to the road at night, with all the dangers that involves (Luke 24:28–29). More than that, in the morning they'd fled Jerusalem in fear of their lives. Now they return to the city. They return because they've seen the good news of Jesus in the Scriptures and they can't keep it to themselves.

5

The Bible is relational

Have you ever wondered why the Bible is so weird? It's not a book I would ever have written. Hundreds of Christian books have been written over the years. None of them is like the Bible. If I'd submitted the Bible as a draft manuscript to one of my editors, they wouldn't have been impressed. It's too long for one thing. It's quite repetitive. They would definitely have told me to take out Chronicles and three of the Gospels. Then there are the bits that are just confusing. I'd have been told it needed a good rewrite.

The problem arises if we assume that the Bible is there to give us information about God. And if that's all there is to it, then it's a weird book because it does that task so slowly and often ambiguously. It would have been so much easier if the Bible had been organized like an encyclopedia with some bullet points along the way. Many large (mostly boring) books on theology seem to have been designed to help us turn the Bible into summaries of truth, as if our job is to tidy up the mess God made of the Bible.

But think about what you do if you want to know someone. Do you give your child your CV? Do you communicate with your spouse through Post-it notes? No, we spend time with people. We listen to their stories. We 'just' chat.

If God were just interested in conveying a few facts, the Bible would be a series of bullet points. But it's not like that: God is interested in relationships. Think how human relationships work. There are times of intense conversation, or occasions when you give a quick summary of important information. But there are also long periods when you tell stories or simply pass the time together. If we're not careful, we can reduce our relationship with God to the spiritual equivalent of speed dating. All the information is crammed into a couple of minutes and then we're on our way.

Imagine I get home from work and my wife starts telling me about her day. Suppose I interrupt by saying, 'Can I stop you there? Could you just give me the one-sentence summary because there are things I'd rather be doing?' That's not a recipe for a good relationship with my wife, and neither is it a good recipe for a good relationship with God! Reading the Bible is about living in relationship with God. And God is not in a hurry.

The Bible is the place where we spend time getting to know God. That means reading the Bible can't be done in a hurry. We can't replace time with God with bullet-point summaries (which can be how we're tempted to use study Bibles and Bible reading notes). We're missing the point of the Bible.

God is known through his words

Suppose someone said, 'I trust Tim Chester completely, but I wouldn't trust a word he says.' What would you make of such a statement? It makes no sense. That's because a person's words are tightly linked to that person. They're not quite the same thing. If you were talking to me on the phone, you wouldn't assume I was in the room just because you could hear my words. But you would assume my words expressed who I am and what I think. Even if you discover that I've been lying, my words are still a revelation of me – in this case a revelation of my bad character. In the same way, the invisible God is known through his words. The attributes ascribed to God's word mirror the attributes of God himself (both are true, light, eternal, powerful, life-giving and so on). Even more striking, perhaps, people show reverence towards God's word as if to God. For example, Psalm 119:120 says, 'My flesh trembles in fear of you; I stand in awe of your laws.' (See also Psalms 56:4, 10; 119:162; Isaiah 66:2, 5.)

This is important. Sometimes people accuse evangelicals of 'bibliolatry' – an idolatry of the Bible in which we place reverence of the Bible alongside the reverence of God. But that assumes a false separation between God and his words (unless, as is usually the case with people making this accus-ation, you don't believe the words of the Bible are the words of God). To trust God's word is to trust God. To disobey God's word is to disobey God. Adam didn't say to God in Genesis 3, 'I know I doubted your word, but I still trust you.' No, he hid from God in shame because he had disobeyed God's word. Tim Ward says,

> To put your trust in the words of the covenant promise
> God makes to you is itself to put your trust in God: the
> two are the same thing. *Communication from* God is therefore
> *communion with* God, when met with a response of trust
> from us.[1]

God is present through his words

The Bible is not primarily a doctrinal book (although we can derive plenty of doctrinal truth from its pages). Primarily it's a *covenantal* book. It's designed not just to impart information about God (though it does do that), but to bring us into a relationship with him. Calvin says, 'We enjoy Christ only as we embrace Christ clad in his own promises.' Again, he says that we receive Christ 'clothed with his gospel'.[2] The Puritan John White said, 'The reading of Scripture is nothing else but a kind of holy conference with God, wherein we enquire after, and he reveals unto us himself, and his will.'[3]

I've recently been working through the Old Testament story with my church, and I've been struck by how God is never seen in the story, but he's always speaking. God is clearly present and active in the life of his people. But his presence is felt through his words. And it's the same for us. We don't see God, but we do experience his presence through his word. In Deuteronomy 30:11–14 Moses says God's word is near us. In Romans 10:6–8 Paul quotes this passage to say that *Christ* is near us. He is near us through his word.

Imagine a small girl waking up in the middle of the night. She cries out for her father. It's dark. She's confused and frightened. And then she hears the voice of her father. 'It's all right, sweetheart. Everything's OK. You go back to sleep.' In the dark she might not actually see him. But the voice of her father is a reassurance of his presence. In the same way, the voice of God in the word of God is a sign of his presence. We not only hear God's voice in his word, we experience God's presence. Calvin said,

> If our Lord is so good to us as to have his doctrine still
> preached to us, we have by that a sure and infallible sign that

he is near at hand to us, that he seeks our salvation, that he
calls us to himself as though he spoke with open mouth, and
that we see him personally before us . . . [Jesus Christ] holds
out his arms to receive us, as often as the gospel is preached
to us . . . Let us assure ourselves that God offers himself to
us in the person of his only Son, when he sends us pastors
and teachers.[4]

Letters are always a bit of problem for movie-makers because
people normally read them quietly. Someone standing quietly
holding a piece of paper doesn't make good cinema, and we,
the viewers, don't know what's being said. One device
directors use to get round this is to have a voiceover with
the letter-writer reading the letter as if he or she were in the
presence of the reader. That's how we should read the Bible.
In our imaginations we should cut away to God speaking a
voiceover as we read. The love letter that God wrote to us
over 2,000 years ago is, as it were, read to us in our presence
by the Holy Spirit.

William Tyndale was martyred because of his commitment
to translating the Bible into English. Why did reading the
Bible matter so much to Tyndale? Here's part of his answer:

God is nothing but his law and his promises . . . God is but his
word, as Christ saith, John viii. 'I am that I say unto you'; that
is to say, That which I preach I am; my words are spirit and life.
God is that only which he testifieth of himself; and to imagine
any other thing of God than that, is damnable idolatry.[5]

It's a bold statement: 'God is but his word.' Tyndale isn't
claiming that God and the Bible are the same thing. He's
saying that it's through his words that we have access to God.
Any other 'version' of God is idolatry. You might say of

someone, 'I know them really well – we've spent hours chatting.' No sensible person would reply, 'Oh, you only know their words; you don't know them.'

One of the most dramatic encounters with the glory of God is surely that experienced by Moses on Mount Sinai. It was so intense that when he came down the mountain, his face was 'radiant'. As a result, he had to veil his face because the sight filled the people with fear. We assume this was because somehow Moses had absorbed the energy emanating from God. But this is not what the Bible says. Exodus 34:29 says that 'his face was radiant because he had *spoken* with the LORD'. Moses encountered the glory of God in the word of God. Think about the implications of that for a moment. If it was the word of God, then maybe we too can encounter God's glory in his word. And that's exactly what Paul says in 2 Corinthians 3:7 – 4:6. We all 'with unveiled faces contemplate the Lord's glory' (3:18). And where do we see it? We see it 'in the light of the gospel that displays the glory of Christ' (4:4). Does that mean your face will glow as Moses' did when you read the Bible? Will you have to buy a veil? No, but your *life* will glow with glory. Paul says, 'And we all, who with unveiled faces contemplate the Lord's glory, are being transformed into his image with ever-increasing glory.'

WYSIWYG

WYSIWYG or 'wiz-ee-wig' is an acronym for 'what you see is what you get'. It describes any computer programme that allows you to see what the end result will look like. It means you don't get any horrible hidden surprises.

God the Father didn't reveal himself in something other than himself. He didn't just write a book. If he had done, we could never be sure that the book was an accurate reflection of God's character. God revealed himself *in his Son*. And because the Father and the Son are one being, *what you see is what you get*.

Then, as we've seen, the Spirit ensured that God's revelation of himself in his Son was accurately recorded in the Bible, and the Spirit also opens our eyes to receive that revelation. The Holy Spirit is also God. So it's not just the objective revelation of God that's divine. Our subjective reception of that revelation is also divine – we understand the Bible through the Spirit. And the Spirit who reveals Christ to us is the Spirit *of* Christ. He knows the mind of God because he *is* God. So *what you hear is what you get*.

What this trinitarian view of Scripture adds up to is this: *we meet God in the Bible*. In the Bible WYSIWYG. The words of the Bible convey God himself and not some distorted or corrupted version of him. God himself in the person of the Spirit ensures that we meet God himself in the person of his Son when we read the Bible. John Frame says,

> *Word* is a title of the second person of the Trinity, and
> whenever one divine person acts in the world, the other two
> persons act together with him. God *is* the word, and the word
> is God. So we conclude that wherever God is, the word is,
> and wherever the word is, God is. Whenever God speaks,
> he himself is there with us.[6]

This doesn't mean that reading the Bible is a mystical process that bypasses our intellect. It's all too easy for us to impose our own ideas and desires on the text and then read them as the voice of God. That's why the objective nature of God's word is important. It's not open to any interpretation. The Bible is the Spirit-inspired authoritative record of God's revelation that judges all our impressions and desires. The Bible means what it says, not what we read into it. So reading it is an intellectual process, not in the sense that it can only be done by intellectuals, but in the sense that we need to use our minds as we read it. Reading the Bible is never *less than* an intellectual process.

But reading the Bible is *more than* an intellectual process. We are not just reading *about* God. We hear the voice of God and encounter his presence through his words.

Get on board

You might be thinking, 'Hang on a minute. I've read a Bible. And it wasn't much fun. Yes, there are some great bits. But a lot of it feels like hard work. Some of it is puzzling. I don't always like what I read. And sometimes it's just dull.'

I have a lot of sympathy with these sentiments. That's how it often feels to me. But I'm not sure we'd get much sympathy from David! David says of God's words:

> They are more precious than gold,
>   than much pure gold;
> they are sweeter than honey,
>   than honey from the honeycomb.
> (Psalm 19:10)

David is talking about the first five books of the Bible. When David writes, there's no Isaiah, there are none of the four Gospels, no letters. There is no Isaiah 53, no John 1, no Romans 8. David's talking about the same Bible we read, but without what we think of as the best bits! Yet David says that it's more precious than gold and sweeter than honey. In Psalm 119 he says, 'My soul is consumed with longing for your laws at all times' (verse 20); 'I have set my heart on your laws' (verse 30); 'I delight in your commands because I love them' (verse 47). David loves God's word, delights in God's word, longs for God's word.

The difference between us and David is not what he was reading. No, the difference is that he had a different attitude to the Bible. In Psalm 119 David begins by talking about 'the law of the LORD' (verse 1). He talks about 'his statutes' and 'his ways' (verses 2–3). But after verse 3, David addresses God directly. He says, 'You have laid down precepts' (verse 4). He goes on to talk about 'your decrees' (verse 5), 'your commands' (verse 6), 'your righteous laws' (verse 7), 'your decrees' (verse 8), 'your word' (verse 9), 'your commands' (verse 10), 'your word' (verse 11), 'your decrees' (verse 12), 'all the laws that come from your mouth' (verse 13), 'your statutes' (verse 14), 'your ways' (verse 15), 'your word' (verse 16). On and on it goes. He never talks about 'the Bible' or 'the word' or 'the Scriptures'. It is always 'your'. David doesn't think he's reading a book of information about God. He's reading *God's* word and hearing *God's* voice. These are the words that 'come from *your* mouth' (verse 13).

'The fulfilment and the end,' says Augustine of the Scriptures, is love for God and love for neighbour. And so we should feel about the Bible the same way we feel about roads: 'We are to love the things by which we are borne only for the sake of that towards which we are borne.'⁷ If I'm away from home, I love it when I get to the A1(M) motorway because it bears me home to my wife. But I don't love it because I'm obsessed with tarmac. I love it because I love my wife. Or, as Tim Ward puts it, we shouldn't be the Christian equivalent of a train-spotter. Train-spotters love trains so much that they collect their serial numbers. That's fine if you like that sort of thing. But that's not what trains are for. Trains are designed to carry you somewhere. In the same way, we don't study the

Bible so we can know a little bit more about Leviticus 18. We read the Bible because it carries us to our Saviour and enables us to live a life that pleases him. So stop being a Christian train-spotter and get on board!

Imagine a young wife whose husband is away, so she phones him every day. Imagine asking her, 'Why do you do that?' Suppose she responds, 'Because I love my phone.' That would be a strange response. Instead, she's going to respond, 'What a stupid question. I love my husband. I love to hear his voice.' But if you then asked her whether she loves her phone, she would say, 'Of course I do because it enables me to hear my husband's voice.'

Now let's change the question: 'Why should you read the Bible?' 'Because I love the Bible' is a strange response. The better response is 'What a stupid question. I love our husband, our Saviour, our Jesus. I love to hear his voice.' But if you're then asked whether you love the Bible, your answer is going to be, 'Of course I do, because it enables me to hear my Saviour's voice.'

Or let's change the analogy. Imagine a mother with a sick child on a dialysis machine. Imagine her cradling her son while he's hooked up to the machine. You ask her, 'Why connect your child to the dialysis machine?' Suppose she responds, 'Because I love this dialysis machine. I find its internal mechanisms fascinating.' That would be a strange response. Instead, the mother is going to respond, 'What a stupid question. I love my child and this machine gives him health and life.' But if you then asked her whether she loved the dialysis machine, she would say, 'Of course I do because it gives life and health to my child.'

My danger is that I love the Bible for its own sake. I love its internal mechanisms. I love its literary structures, its allusions and its rhetoric. That's OK. But if that's my only focus, then

I might as well be an English literature teacher analysing the plays of Shakespeare. We love the Bible because it gives us health and life.

In chapter 1 we saw how John begins his first letter by describing how he was ensuring that his readers had the apostolic testimony in written form (1 John 1:1–4). But why? Is John just setting the record straight? Is he a historian obsessed with historical facts? No, he has a bigger purpose in mind:

> We proclaim to you what we have seen and heard, so that you also may have fellowship with us. And our fellowship is with the Father and with his Son, Jesus Christ. We write this to make our joy complete.
>
> (1 John 1:3–4)

John writes so that we too can share this fellowship or relationship with the Father and Son. We may not be able physically to see and hear and touch Jesus. But through the Spirit of God we see him and hear him and touch him in the word of God. And so we share with John the joy of knowing God.

Have a plan, but don't make the plan the point

We don't create our relationship with God. It's not something we achieve. It's given to us by grace. But we are involved in our *experience* of the relationship. We receive from God and respond to him. For a relationship to thrive, we need to spend time talking with people. And our relationship with God is no different. We need to spend time hearing him in his word and responding in prayer. So arrange your time so that you can read the Bible every day. And adopt a plan to help you read through the Bible.

But whatever plan you adopt, it's essential to realize that completing the plan is not what is important. This is not about ticking off a list. It's not about winning the approval of God or other people. God in his grace is always well disposed towards us.

Imagine I go away and promise to phone my wife every day. Suppose I miss a day. How would my wife feel if the next day I said, 'I'm going to ring off now, but I'll ring you back straight away. I'm going to phone you twice today because I didn't phone you yesterday.' She would say, 'I don't want you to phone me so that you can tick me off a list. I want you to phone because you want to talk with me.' But she might also say, 'I do want you to phone tomorrow!'

So don't worry if you fall behind with a Bible reading plan. The point of the exercise is not completing the plan or proving yourself as a Christian. The point is to hear God's voice. God isn't interested in whether you're up to date. He's interested in speaking to you. Quickly skimming several chapters to catch up isn't going to achieve this. So if you fall behind, just miss some chapters out or let yourself be a few days behind. The important thing is to meet with God each day. And every day you can begin again. Take your time. It's better prayerfully to meditate on a few verses than mindlessly turn many pages.

Pray the word

A great way to have communion with God as you read the Bible is to turn what you read into prayer. Turn God's speech into a two-way conversation. Worship over the word. I used to read my Bible in the morning and then pray through what I'd read as I walked to work.

One way of doing this is to read the passage as a whole and then reread a verse or two at a time. After each section, turn what you've read into prayer. You might respond with praise or confession or thanksgiving or with a request. In the case of a story, you might focus on two or three verses that capture your attention or summarize God's involvement. Think of the process as being like that of an animal sniffing out nutritious food in the undergrowth, or a child snuggling into the side of her father.

Let's look at Psalm 19 as an example, since it's also a psalm about the word of God:

> The heavens declare the glory of God;
>> the skies proclaim the work of his hands.
> Day after day they pour forth speech;
>> night after night they reveal knowledge.
> They have no speech, they use no words;
>> no sound is heard from them.
> Yet their voice goes out into all the earth,
>> their words to the ends of the world.
> (verses 1–4a)

You might identify some beautiful things you've seen recently and give thanks for them, acknowledging that they reveal the goodness and greatness of God. You might ask God to make you more aware of the way the world communicates his glory:

> In the heavens God has pitched a tent for the sun.
>> It is like a bridegroom coming out of his chamber,
>> like a champion rejoicing to run his course.
> It rises at one end of the heavens
>> and makes its circuit to the other;
>> nothing is deprived of its warmth.
> (verses 4b–6)

You might thank God for the life-giving warmth of the sun. As you thank God for his care over the world, you might also pray for some of the needs of the world that you've heard about in the news:

> The law of the Lord is perfect,
>> refreshing the soul.
> The statutes of the Lord are trustworthy,
>> making wise the simple.
> The precepts of the Lord are right,
>> giving joy to the heart.
> The commands of the Lord are radiant,
>> giving light to the eyes.
> The fear of the Lord is pure,
>> enduring for ever.
> The decrees of the Lord are firm,
>> and all of them are righteous.
> They are more precious than gold,
>> than much pure gold;
> they are sweeter than honey,
>> than honey from the honeycomb.
> (verses 7–10)

You might thank God for his precious and sweet word. You might pray that as you read the Bible today, it would refresh your soul. You might pray that the preaching in your church would give light to people's eyes. It may be that you have a decision to make, so you might pray that God would make you wise. You might pray that people you know who are struggling would be given joy through God's word:

> By them your servant is warned;
>> in keeping them there is great reward.

But who can discern their own errors?
(verses 11–12a)

You might ask God to warn you of sin and reveal to you any sin of which you're unaware. You might ask the Spirit to lead you to your great reward in Christ so that the enticements of sin grow weak:

> Forgive my hidden faults.
> Keep your servant also from wilful sins;
>   may they not rule over me.
> Then I will be blameless,
>   innocent of great transgression.
> (verses 12b–13)

You might use this as an opportunity to confess your sin and ask God to help you keep in step with the Spirit:

> May these words of my mouth and this meditation
>   of my heart
>   be pleasing in your sight,
>   LORD, my Rock and my Redeemer.
> (verse 14)

You might ask God to help you meditate on what you've read in his word throughout the day. You might ask him to ensure your speech is wholesome. You might ask for opportunities to share God's word with unbelievers. You might end by praising God, our Rock and our Redeemer.

6

The Bible is intentional

Consider the following words:

1. 'In 1966 England won the football World Cup.'
2. 'Jonny, I won't tell you again. It's time for you to go to bed.'

What happens next?

With the first statement the answer could well be nothing. Perhaps your team goes on to win the pub quiz. But those words don't carry any intent. They're not designed to *do* anything – other than convey some information.

But it's a different story with the second statement. Something is going to happen next. The words are not actually a command. Like the first statement, they simply convey information. But that information has clear implications. The words of this second statement have intent. They're designed to produce a result. Indeed, they inevitably *will* produce a result. What happens next is going to be either an act of obedience or some form of disobedience. Ideally, Jonny will go to bed. But maybe he won't, in which case the outcome will be parental discipline. We can't be sure what will happen, but *something* will happen. Jonny is not going to go on watching the television undisturbed.

The point is this: some words *describe* reality and some words *shape* reality.

Think about the words: 'I love you.' Again, technically they're just descriptive. But if they're said for the first time by a young man to a young woman, then they may create a cross-roads in their relationship. Depending on her response, their friendship may either blossom into romance or die an awkward death. What's clear is that once those words have left his mouth, nothing between them will ever be the same again.

What about the Bible? At first sight there's a combination of both describing words and shaping words. Narrative sections tell stories. They're descriptions of historical events. Meanwhile, once commandments have been heard, they inevitably change reality, by leading either to obedience or to disobedience. So at first sight the Bible looks like a mix of describing words and shaping words.

But in fact the whole Bible is written with intent. *All* its words are designed to shape reality – even the descriptions. Like the words to Jonny in our second statement, even the descriptions in the Bible carry implications. One way or another, they call us to faith and repentance. God's words shape and reshape reality: 'The Christian revelation not only discloses information about God's character; it also reasserts his rule over a wayward and rebellious people.'[1]

The pattern is set right from the beginning. Into the emptiness God speaks, and his words create reality. Atoms and molecules form through his words. And into the primordial chaos God speaks, and his words reshape reality. He separates light and dark, sea and land. He creates order, beauty and life.

God's words are spoken with intent. He has a purpose for them. When God calls the prophet Jeremiah, he tells him, 'I have put my words in your mouth. See, today I appoint you over nations and kingdoms to uproot and tear down, to destroy and overthrow, to build and to plant' (Jeremiah 1:9–10); '"Is not my word like fire," declares the LORD, "and like a hammer that breaks a rock in pieces?"' (Jeremiah 23:29). God's word through Jeremiah will uproot and plant, destroy and build.

Psalm 29 is a wonderful depiction of the power of God's voice:

> The voice of the LORD is over the waters;
>> the God of glory thunders,
>> the LORD thunders over the mighty waters.
> The voice of the LORD is powerful;
>> the voice of the LORD is majestic.
> The voice of the LORD breaks the cedars;
>> the LORD breaks in pieces the cedars of Lebanon.
> He makes Lebanon leap like a calf,
>> Sirion like a young wild ox.
> The voice of the LORD strikes
>> with flashes of lightning.
> The voice of the LORD shakes the desert;
>> the LORD shakes the Desert of Kadesh.
> The voice of the LORD twists the oaks
>> and strips the forests bare.
> And in his temple all cry, 'Glory!'
> (Psalm 29:3–9)

If you opened your Bible this morning, this was what was unleashed! God's word has power and, because it has power, God's word always achieves what he intends:

As the rain and the snow
    come down from heaven,
and do not return to it
    without watering the earth
and making it bud and flourish,
    so that it yields seed for the sower
        and bread for the eater,
so is my word that goes out from my mouth:
    it will not return to me empty,
but will accomplish what I desire
    and achieve the purpose for which I sent it.
(Isaiah 55:10–11)

The Bible is never simply a record of events or ideas. It is always intentional. Here's how Tim Ward puts it:

> In Scripture, God presents himself to us, making his covenant promise to us. As part of that overall action, he performs many subsidiary actions through Scripture: eliciting faith, warning, rebuking, encouraging, provoking hope, motivating to repentance and holiness and so on. And, as a necessary feature of all these actions, God teaches us truth about himself, ourselves, the past and the future. Thus Scripture, like all spoken or written language, is made up of propositional content and authorial purpose, and the two ought never to be separated if we wish to hear what God is saying in Scripture.
>
> Therefore the most appropriate question to ask ourselves when we open Scripture to read it is: *What is God wanting to do to me, and in me, through the words I am reading?* When we read the Bible we must be ready, in the first instance, for God to *act* on us and in us. For, as we encounter his words, and as we encounter the actions he performs by means of them, we are encountering God himself.[2]

Asking the 'Why?' question

The fact that God intends to speak through, and meet us in, his word affects how we approach the Bible. There are three players involved when we read the Bible: the author, the text and the reader. An evangelical understanding of the Bible identifies the meaning of a passage with the meaning intended by the authors – both the human author and the divine author (even if Old Testament writers didn't always fully appreciate how what they wrote would be fulfilled). That's because we see Scripture as an act of divine communication. God intends to speak, and therefore we intend to hear his voice. He has a purpose just as surely as a father does when he tells his daughter to come in for dinner. The father isn't playing with words or inviting his daughter to interpret his words as she chooses. And our heavenly Father is no different when he speaks.

Texts and readers still matter. The meaning intended by God is conveyed through human authors in the text of the Bible. So our job is to identify the meaning God intends by playing close attention to the text. But we mustn't get so absorbed with the intricacies of the text that we lose sight of the message its human and divine authors intended. Readers matter as well. As readers, we come with our own assumptions and we need to pay attention to these. But this doesn't mean that the text means whatever it means to me. Quite the opposite, in fact. We're alert to our own perspectives, so those perspectives can be challenged by God through his word. We want to avoid our prejudices distorting our reading of the Bible. So we pay attention to the text and ourselves as readers *so that* we can hear the message intended by the human and divine authors.

This means that as we read the Bible, it's really important to ask the 'Why?' question as well as the 'What?' question:

'Why is it being said?', as well as 'What is being said?' This principle applies to Bible books, stories, sections, paragraphs and sentences. You can even apply it to words within sentences. So we ask ourselves questions like: Why was this book written? What was the intention of the author? Why did he include this section or paragraph? What does this sentence add to the argument? Why is this detail included? Why did he write it in this way? What outcome does he hope to produce? How does he want to shape or reshape his hearers?

Sometimes people identify a number of truths in a passage and then apply those truths to similar situations today. That's OK. But if that's all they do, then it's a missed opportunity. They've asked the 'What?' question ('What does this passage mean?'). But without the 'Why?' question, we don't get the sense of purpose. We don't hear the application intended by the original divine and human authors. We hear truth from the Bible. But we blunt its power to bring change.

Asking the 'Why?' question of Bible books

We've seen that the Bible was written *for us*. But it wasn't written *to us*. It always has an original audience in mind. So we need to work out why the original authors were writing it to their original audience.

As children, we used to play a game in our family. Whenever the phone rang, we'd try to work out who was calling from the responses of the person who'd picked up the receiver. Reading the Bible can be a little like this. We have one end of the conversation. But it helps to form some idea of what was going on at the other end of the line. Think of each book of the Bible as half a conversation. We need to use this to reconstruct the other half of the conversation. Who is writing to whom? What are their situations? Do they mention specific problems?

Sometimes it's fairly obvious what the intent of a Bible book is. Paul didn't write 1 Corinthians because he was bored and thought it might be fun to catch up with the Corinthians. The church in Corinth was in a bit of mess. So Paul writes with a sense of urgency to sort things out. There is a list of issues he needs to address, and he works through them one by one.

But what about 1 and 2 Kings (which was originally one book)? Is Kings just a description of historical events? The history books of the Bible are never *less* than history: that is, they provide an accurate and reliable account of historical events. But they're always *more* than history. They have a purpose beyond simply recording what happened. They're story plus explanation, or history with theological annotations.

There were other accounts of the period covered by the book of Kings. The book makes reference to other historical sources, such as 'the annals of Solomon' (1 Kings 11:41) and 'the annals of the kings of Judah' (1 Kings 14:29; 15:7). Yet the writer clearly decided to write a new account. And this involved carefully selecting his material. So there are some long reigns which are hardly mentioned because they're tangential to his purpose.

So what was that purpose? Kings was written after Jerusalem had fallen to the Babylonians. The people are in exile. The king is in captivity. The temple is in ruins. The land is under foreign rule. So it looks for all the world like the promises of God have run into the ground. It's a time of social, cultural and theological crisis. We get a sense of that emotional dislocation in the book of Lamentations. So Kings addresses the questions of the exiles: Are the gods of Babylon stronger than the Lord? Have God's promises failed? Has God abandoned his people? Are his people beyond hope?

The response of Kings is summarized in God's word to
Solomon in 1 Kings 9. Verses 7–8 summarize the questions
being asked by the first readers: 'Why has the LORD done such
a thing to this land and to this temple?' Verse 9 is the answer:
'Because they have forsaken the LORD their God, who brought
their ancestors out of Egypt, and have embraced other gods,
worshipping and serving them – that is why the LORD brought
all this disaster on them.'

But the writer also offers hope. If God's word of judgment
has proved certain, then so will God's word of promise.
Throughout the story, the writer highlights fulfilments
of God's promises. He highlights confrontations between
the king and God's word or prophet in which God's word
wins every time. God's word is sovereign in history. The
sovereignty of God's word is *bad news* because the law of
Moses spoke of curses that would befall God's people if
they were unfaithful. But its sovereignty is also *good news*
because God promised David a king over his people for
ever. Woven into the narrative are stories of life from death.
To a nation with no future, they function as a promise of
new life.

So Kings is a book of history. But it's more than history. It
has a theological agenda as well. And the writer has a number
of devices for promoting this agenda:

- *Editorial selection:* the writer has chosen what to
  include and what to omit from his sources.
- *Divine speech:* direct words from God provide
  a divine perspective on history as we saw with
  1 Kings 9:3–9.
- *Royal summaries:* the writer provides a summary of
  most kings at the beginning and end of their reign,
  which includes an evaluation of the king.

- *Editorial comment:* in addition to the evaluation of each king, there are other instances of editorial comment (1 Kings 21:25–26; 2 Kings 17:7–23; 18:12; 24:20).
- *Paradigms:* David is promoted as a paradigm of a good king, while Jeroboam is a negative paradigm.
- *Parallels:* the writer places stories side by side so they explain each other.
- *Comparison with the nations:* God had expelled the Canaanites from the land because of their idolatry and injustice. The writer of Kings draws attention to the fact that now God's people are doing similar things with a similar result (1 Kings 21:25–26; 2 Kings 21:9).

Asking the 'Why?' question of stories and sections

What about individual stories or sections? In Mark 4:35 – 5:43, Mark recounts four miracles. The 'What?' question is fairly straightforward: Jesus calms a storm, restores a demon-possessed man, heals a woman and raises a twelve-year-old girl from the dead. But if you stop there, then it will not be clear what we're to make of this passage. You might conclude that if you're ever caught in a storm and Jesus is asleep in the boat with you, then you should wake him up. But that's not a situation any of us are ever going to face. Or you might decide that if your daughter dies, then you should ask Jesus to raise her from the dead. But it's a conclusion that will probably lead to bitter disappointment. That's not the point Mark has in mind.

So let's ask the 'Why?' question. Why has Mark selected these parables and included them at this point in his Gospel? And why has he told them in the way he has done?

Jesus has just been teaching about the kingdom of God (Mark 4:1–34). The four parables then highlight the authority of Jesus over the natural world, the spirit world, sickness and death. So taken together and read in context, they reveal Jesus as God's King. Not only that, in each story Mark contrasts fear and faith (4:40; 5:15, 33–34, 36). He presents us with a choice. We can respond to the evidence of Jesus' identity with fear or with faith. So faith here doesn't involve believing my sickness will be healed or my child raised to life. It means trusting that Jesus is the King who will establish God's kingdom – a kingdom without sickness or death. The 'punchline' is 5:36: 'Don't be afraid, just believe.'

Or consider Paul's famous words about love in 1 Corinthians 13:4–9: 'Love is patient, love is kind' and so on. If we just ask the 'What?' question, then we have a beautiful description of love – ideal for reading at weddings and putting on greetings cards. But what if we ask the 'Why?' question? Paul is addressing a divided church (1:10–13; 3:1–23). The immediate context is a discussion of the pride and jealousy caused by the Corinthian church's attitude to spiritual gifts. Here are people looking down on others because they lack certain spiritual gifts or are using their gifts in a selfish way. Suddenly Paul's description of love becomes a stinging rebuke. Paul doesn't want his readers to go, 'How lovely' as these verses are read. He hopes they will go hang their heads in shame.

Asking the 'Why?' question of the way the Bible is written

The kind of reaction writers want to produce is often reflected in the way they write. So we can also ask the 'Why?' question of the way something is written. Is the language designed to evoke wonder, fear, laughter or confidence?

In the parable of the prodigal son, a younger son squanders his father's inheritance. But when he repents, he's welcomed home. It's a picture of our heavenly Father's grace. But his elder brother is angry because his hard work suddenly appears to have gained him no advantage and so he refuses to join the celebrations. The parable ends with the father going out to plead with the elder brother. 'We had to celebrate and be glad,' he says, 'because this brother of yours was dead and is alive again; he was lost and is found' (Luke 15:32). Can you remember what happens next? Does the elder brother respond to his father's plea and join the celebration, or does he reject his father's grace and remain outside the party?

Of course, it's a trick question. For the parable just ends with the father's plea, and we never get to find out what the elder brother does next. What's Jesus up to? What's his intent? Jesus stops the story at this point, so we're left asking, 'What will the elder brother do next?' 'How will the Pharisees respond?' and 'What would I do?' We're subtly drawn into the story. Instead of simply being passive observers, we find that we're participants. The story implicates us. We realize that we can't simply listen to the tale to be entertained. It forces us to decide how *we* will respond to God's grace. Are we going to join God's party or are we going to remain outside?

We can even ask the 'Why?' question of individual words. In Mark's account of the feeding of the 5,000 we read, 'Then Jesus told them to make all the people sit down in groups on the green grass' (Mark 6:39). The meaning of the sentence is clear. But why does Mark include the word 'green'? What other kind of grass is there? Is Mark really worried we might think the grass was red? The answer, I think, is that Mark has in mind Psalm 23:

> The LORD is my shepherd, I lack nothing.
>   He makes me lie down in *green* pastures.

In verse 34 Mark has already told us that Jesus had compassion on the crowd because 'they were like sheep without a shepherd'. So the green grass reinforces the claim that Jesus is the LORD, come to shepherd his people.

A covenant book

Let's return to the young man we met at the beginning of the chapter who said 'I love you' to a young woman. And let's suppose that two years later they're standing in front of their family and friends, saying to each other, 'I do'. What happens next? A minister says, 'I therefore proclaim that they are husband and wife. Those whom God has joined together let no one put asunder.' As a result of those words a new reality exists – a marriage. That single man is no longer single. His identity has radically changed. He's now a married man. For the young woman, that change of identity probably involves a change of name. Miss Freeman has become Mrs Chester. The couple are now bound together in a covenant, and that covenant has been created by their words.

The Bible is a covenant document. It creates covenant relationships. It's not just that it describes covenants – as it does in Exodus 24:7, for example, which speaks of 'the Book of the Covenant'. It is itself a covenant-making word. The phrase 'the Book of the Covenant' is also used in 2 Chronicles 34:29–32, and here it describes a larger portion of Scripture and possibly *all* of what was then regarded as Scripture. The Bible is 'the Book of the Covenant'. There's actually a clue in the name of its two parts. We call them the Old and New Testaments, and 'testament' is an old word for 'covenant'.

At the heart of any covenant is a *promise*. In the covenant of marriage we promise 'to have and to hold, from this day forward, for better, for worse, for richer, for poorer, in sickness and in health, to love and to cherish, till death do us part'. In and through the Bible God makes promises to us.

But a covenant is more than a promise. It's also a *contract*. A marriage is legally binding. You can only undo a marriage by seeking a divorce through the courts. In the Bible we have God's promises 'in writing'. In the Bible God makes a promise to which he is then committed.

But a covenant is also more than a contract. Marriage is not just a commitment to carry on loving one another. It changes the nature of your relationship. As a result of the marriage covenant, a man stops being single and becomes a husband. A wife may change her name. Covenants bind people together in a *relationship*. It's the same with God's covenants. God's covenant changes our identity. If you respond to God's covenant promises in the Bible with faith, then your identity is changed. You become part of God's people and God becomes your God. Reading and rereading the Bible with faith reinforces that covenant identity and covenant security.

The Bible, then, is intentional in the sense that it's written with intent. God uses the Bible to achieve his purposes. We've met some of those purposes already, but let's summarize what God does through the Bible as it's read and taught:

- God gives life through his word.
- God judges the world through his word.
- God reassures his people through his word.
- God trains his servants through his word.
- God rules his church through his word.

Above all, God uses the Bible to enter into a covenant relationship with those who are his people. Kevin Vanhoozer says,

The Spirit speaking in Scripture continues the threefold office of Christ (as Prophet, Priest and King); witnessing to the truth of the living and written word; executing the . . . force of Scripture so that it reigns in the hearts and lives of believers; mediating the personal presence of Christ through the words that testify to him to bring about personal union with Christ.[3]

Expectant readers

What does the intentionality of the Bible mean for us as readers? It means we need to read with expectation. If the Bible is written with a purpose in mind, then we need to expect it to achieve that purpose. We need to expect the Bible to bring both life and death as it's proclaimed. We need to expect the Bible to both comfort and challenge us. We need to respond with faith when the Bible reassures us and with obedience when it directs us.

There'll be many times when you read the Bible and think, 'I don't understand everything that's going on here.' 'I'm not feeling anything special as I read.' 'This doesn't feel like a moment of glory.' But all the time God's word will be shaping your character and your affections. How many of the meals you have eaten throughout your life do you remember? The chances are it's only a handful. Was it therefore pointless eating all those meals? Of course not. They've nourished and sustained you. Sometimes people liken reading the Bible to pouring water through a sieve. What's the point of that? But while you may not end up with a sieve full of water, you do end up with a clean sieve. Remember: the Bible is a busy book. When it's read, God is at work.

7

The Bible is enough

Jesus once told a parable. A rich man lived in luxury while at his gate lived a poor beggar named Lazarus. When they died, Lazarus was carried by angels to Abraham's side. But the rich man was in torment in hell. In the parable the rich man sees Abraham with Lazarus at his side and calls on Abraham to send Lazarus to 'dip the tip of his finger in water and cool my tongue'. But it can't be done because 'a great chasm has been set in place' between heaven and hell. The warning is clear: there is life after death, and your eternal future is irrevocably set in this life. In the light of these great truths, we need to see the spiritual danger of money. Just before he told this parable, Jesus said, 'You cannot serve both God and Money' (Luke 16:13–26).

And that might be that. But Jesus doesn't stop there. The parable has a strange final twist. The rich man says to Abraham,

' "Then I beg you, father, send Lazarus to my family, for I have five brothers. Let him warn them, so that they will not also come to this place of torment."

'Abraham replied, "They have Moses and the Prophets; let them listen to them."

' "No, father Abraham," he said, "but if someone from the dead goes to them, they will repent."

'He said to him, "If they do not listen to Moses and the Prophets, they will not be convinced even if someone rises from the dead." '

(Luke 16:27–31)

The parable is a warning to repent before it's too late, and the rich man wants that warning to be heard by his five brothers. But Abraham says they can *already* hear the warning. They have it in 'Moses and the Prophets'. As we've seen, that was a common way of referring to the Scriptures. All the information we need for salvation is found in the Bible. And it's not as if it's tucked away in the small print. The Bible is one long plea to sinners to turn back to God and find joy, life and hope in him. The Bible is God's appeal to us. It is, as we've seen, an intentional book, and God has made it fit for purpose.

But the rich man doesn't think it's enough. He wants more. ' "No, father Abraham," he said, "but if someone from the dead goes to them, they will repent." ' He flatly contradicts Abraham. You can see the logic of his position. The Bible is not dramatic enough, not dynamic enough, not exciting enough. But a miracle – that would surely do the job. Someone risen from the dead would convince people.

But Abraham – or rather Jesus – won't budge. The problem is not any deficiency in the Bible. The problem is that people refuse to listen to its message. And if they ignore the Bible, then they'll ignore someone from the dead as well. Indeed, often the miracles of Jesus created fair-weather followers who left him when things got hard (John 6:26, 66).

We need the Bible to do mission. 'Faith comes from hearing the message, and the message is heard through the word about Christ' (Romans 10:17). This doesn't mean you need to carry a Bible with you every time you do evangelism. But you do need to ensure that the words you proclaim are founded in the Scriptures. And you don't need anything else. If you just proclaim words based on the words of the Scriptures, then God's Spirit can use this to save people. The Bible is enough because Jesus is enough. So the Bible is necessary and sufficient. In contrast, miracles are neither necessary nor sufficient. In other words, people can be saved without seeing a miracle, and seeing a miracle is never enough – people also need to hear the message of Christ crucified.

Everything we need

Peter addresses the sufficiency of Scripture and this issue in 2 Peter 1:3–9:

> His divine power has given us everything we need for a godly life through our knowledge of him who called us by his own glory and goodness. Through these he has given us his very great and precious promises, so that through them you may participate in the divine nature, having escaped the corruption in the world caused by evil desires.
>
> For this very reason, make every effort to add to your faith goodness; and to goodness, knowledge; and to knowledge, self-control; and to self-control, perseverance; and to perseverance, godliness; and to godliness, mutual affection; and to mutual affection, love. For if you possess these qualities in increasing measure, they will keep you from being ineffective and unproductive in your knowledge of our Lord Jesus Christ. But whoever does not have them is short-sighted

and blind, forgetting that they have been cleansed from their past sins.

Verse 3 says God has given us everything we need for life and godliness. But what has he given us? There are several ways we could answer that. But the answer Peter gives in verse 4 is that God has given us 'his very great and precious promises'. The repetition of the words 'has given us' in verses 3 and 4 reinforce this link. We have everything we need in the promises of God. And how has God given us his promises? In the Bible. So we have everything we need in the Bible.

The Bible doesn't contain enough information to build a car or find your way to London. When we say we believe the Bible is sufficient, we need to be clear what we think it's sufficient for. Peter says we have all we need for 'a godly life'. There are some issues on which the Bible is not clear. And perhaps that means they're not important to a godly life. But it does contain all we need to know and obey God.

Enough information

Scientific discoveries are advancing all the time. The sum of human knowledge grows year by year. And in recent decades science has begun exploring human psychology. Meanwhile, genetic studies are identifying how our DNA has an impact on our characteristics. It's easy for Christians to get caught up in this and think that to grow as Christians we need to apply to the latest insights of sociology, psychology and psychiatry.

It would be foolish to dismiss such insights. As Christians, we believe God made an ordered world which is therefore open to scientific investigation. And there's no reason why this shouldn't also apply to human beings. We can learn from the secular world.

But we also need to recognize that human affections and thinking are not neutral territory. It's not quite the same as studying weather patterns or chemical reactions. We all have vested interests in this research. Human beings are determined to live independently of God. Peter speaks of 'evil desires' in verse 4. Our evil desires twist our reason. We find ways to justify our pride and selfishness. We have an inbuilt tendency to blame our problems on anything other than our sin. We refuse to admit we're accountable to God or dependent on him. So scientific findings are not as neutral as people portray them. It's this 'corruption in the world' that Christians have escaped (verse 4).

We can go further. Whatever insights human research might add to our knowledge, we have knowledge from the Creator. The Bible is God's word and so it provides God's perspective on human beings. And human beings haven't changed. Human beings in the twenty-first century are not fundamentally different from human beings in the first century. Jesus says, 'Scripture cannot be broken' (John 10:35, ESV). When Scripture doesn't match our experience, we tend to assume that Scripture must be at fault. But, suggests Andrew Wilson, 'Maybe I'm the one who is broken, rather than the Bible.'[1]

Have you ever had to assemble flat-pack furniture? We bought a wardrobe for my daughter. When it arrived, I unpacked everything. The long thin pieces were obviously the sides. They seemed to fit into some top pieces. Gradually it took shape. But then I found there were panels I couldn't fit, shelves the wrong way round, screws left over and bolts that were missing. It had all gone horribly wrong, and I was railing against the incompetence of the manufacturers. Then I noticed in amongst the packaging a set of instructions. Suddenly it became clear that I'd assembled it wrongly. Only once I'd taken everything apart and put it together again using the instructions, did we finish with a beautiful, functional wardrobe.

The Bible contains, as it were, the Maker's instructions for human beings. God knows us better than we know ourselves. And we have his diagnosis of the human condition in the Bible. So it's his word that enables us to be beautiful, functional people. 'The heart,' says Jeremiah, 'is deceitful above all things and beyond cure. Who can understand it?' To which God adds, 'I the LORD search the heart and examine the mind' (Jeremiah 17:9–10). We shouldn't be intimidated by people with letters after their name claiming to explain human behaviour. We need to be tenacious in our commitment to the sufficiency of the Bible.

Here's Peter Adam's list of examples of adding to God's word. I wonder which your greatest danger is:

- The Roman Catholic Church accepts the Bible, and then adds to it the traditions of the church to form one word of God.
- Some conservative evangelical Christians tend to add the middle-class culture and attitudes of the 1920s to the Bible without noticing what they are doing.
- Some Pentecostal churches accept the Bible and add to it some recent words from the Spirit.
- Legalistic evangelicals expand the Bible by adding some useful rules about how we should behave.
- Many denominations hold to their cherished denominational traditions even more firmly than they hold to the Bible.
- Liberal Christians hold on to recent insights from current thought, even when they contradict the Bible.

- Many congregations hold to their cherished traditions even more firmly than they hold to the Bible.
- Many Christian subcultures unconsciously add to the Bible their own assumptions and prejudices.[2]

Enough resources

Let's go back to my flat-pack wardrobe. Suppose I'd laid everything out on the floor and sat down to read the instructions. I have everything I need for a wardrobe. An hour later my wife walks into the room and asks, 'Where's the wardrobe?' 'There,' I say, 'on the floor, and here are the instructions.' 'That's not a wardrobe,' she would reply, 'that's a pile of bits.' And once again I can't blame the manufacturers. I have everything I need. I just need to get on with it.

In the same way, it's not enough simply to sit and read the Bible. Peter applies these truths by urging us to expand our virtues: adding to our faith goodness, knowledge, self-control, perseverance, godliness, mutual affection and love. We need to get on with the job.

But the key thing to realize is this: because we have everything we need, there's nothing holding us back. Peter says we have everything we need from 'his divine power'.

Some Christians believe there's a distinctive and specific second blessing that propels us into greater assurance and holiness. And it's certainly true that Christians sometimes enjoy powerful experiences of God's Spirit. But we already have everything we need: the promise of God and the presence of his Spirit. None of us is waiting for something to happen before we can really grow as Christians.

Imagine being told to wash a car, but not being given any water. How frustrating would that be? It would be an unfair expectation. God, says Peter, has called us to live godly lives

(2 Peter 1:3). We're called by God's glory and goodness to live for his glory and imitate his goodness. But God hasn't left us, as it were, with a dirty car and no water. He's given us everything we need to fulfil the calling to which he's called us.

Growing by knowing

So what is it that enables Christians to grow? The answer is 'knowledge'. Verse 2 says that grace and peace are ours in abundance, 'through the *knowledge* of God and of Jesus our Lord'. Verse 3 says we have 'everything we need for a godly life through our *knowledge* of him'. Verse 8 says we acquire Christian virtues and lead productive Christian lives 'in [our] *knowledge* of our Lord Jesus Christ'. We grow as we know.

So is Peter saying that we grow by reading the Bible? Not quite. It's not that God rewards our efforts in Bible reading by giving us a bit more godliness. The Bible is not a magic book. It's not that twenty chapters of Bible reading give you twenty units of holiness. It's God's great and precious promises that change us. It's the story of the death and resurrection of Jesus. It's the promise of life and hope in his name. It's the transforming presence of the Holy Spirit. It's the new identity we have in the gospel. It's the assurance of God's love. It's the hope of a new creation. It's our adoption as God's children. But where do we find these great and precious promises? In the Bible. Our faith is created, sustained and grows as we encounter God's promises there.

This knowledge is not simply knowledge of facts. This is not mere data or information. In each case these verses speak of the knowledge *of a person*. Remember, the Bible is not just information about God. We meet God in his word. We grow by knowing Jesus better. We shouldn't confuse knowing lots of Bible verses or reading lots of theological books with the kind of knowledge that leads to godliness. Think about what it means for me to know my wife. It involves a lot more than simply knowing things about her. It's much more intimate and personal. It involves developing a relationship with her.

Nevertheless, knowing about God and knowing God go together. The facts of the Christian faith are important. A focus on knowing the person of Jesus is never a mandate for theological ignorance. Knowing information about someone and knowing someone personally are not alternatives. They go together. To know my wife well I need to know when her birthday is and what food she likes. I need to know what she thinks and what pleases her. It's the same with my knowledge of God. My relationship with him involves far more than the accumulation of facts. But it's never less than this. I need to know what he thinks and what pleases him. No wonder then that one of the virtues Peter urges us to acquire is 'knowledge' (verse 5). Our knowledge of God is the foundation for these virtues, but it's also one of the virtues we build on that foundation. Think of it as a virtuous spiral.

Notice, too, what it is that makes a Christian *ineffective* and *unproductive*. Verse 9 says, 'But whoever does not have them is short-sighted and blind, forgetting that they have been cleansed from their past sins.' We stop growing when we forget the precious promises of the Bible. Such a person, says Peter, is short-sighted, blind and forgetful:

- A short-sighted person cannot see the future.
- A blind person cannot see the present.
- A forgetful person cannot see the past.

The Bible is a remedy for all three. The Bible reminds us what God did for us in the past through the cross and resurrection. The Bible reminds us what God is doing for us in the present through the Holy Spirit. And the Bible reminds us what God has in store for us in the future. So we can live now as those whose sins are forgiven, whose identity is secure and whose future is glorious. The result is godliness (verse 3), productivity (verse 8), confidence (verse 10) and endurance (verses 10–11).

Growing by remembering

So knowledge of Jesus through the promise of the Bible is what makes Christians and grows Christians. And the thing that impedes Christian growth is forgetting those promises.

So it will come, then, as no surprise to find that Peter defines the task of Christian leaders as being one of reminding people of God's word. The remedy for forgetting is reminding. He talks of 'reminding' in verse 12, 'refreshing the memory' in verse 13 (it's the same root word as 'remind' in verse 12) and enabling people to 'remember' in verse 15.

Peter's priority is not passing on new knowledge. His readers already know everything they need for godliness (verse 4), and they're firmly established in the truth (verse 12). The primary task of a preacher is not to give people new information. Most of our content will be familiar to most of our hearers. Of course, if there are unbelievers or new believers present, then much of what the preacher says may be new to them. And every believer acquires new information from time to time. But if we make passing on new information the goal of our preaching, then we'll have a dangerous tendency to search out novelty. Our job, instead, is to tell the old, old story (though hopefully in fresh ways). That's because what we're really interested in is *personal* knowledge. We want people to know Jesus, and that means constantly bringing them to him. Peter has urged his readers to 'make every effort' to acquire Christian virtues in verse 5 and make their election sure in verse 10. But for this to happen, he must 'make every effort' to ensure they remember the words of the Bible (verse 15).

You may not be a preacher. But the same principles apply to your Bible reading. Your primary aim is not to seek out new or novel ideas (although you may meet some new ideas as you read). You aim to hear God's voice and meet him in his word.

We find the same emphasis in chapter 3. Peter gives 'reminders' to his readers so they can 'recall' the words of Scripture. He warns them about people who mock God's promises (3:4) and 'deliberately forget' the power of 'God's word' (3:5). He tells his readers not to 'forget' that God's timescales are different from ours (3:8). Since everything we need is wrapped up in the promises of God's word (1:4), Peter now assures us that 'the Lord is not slow in keeping his promise' (3:9). And Peter ends with a final exhortation to 'grow in the grace and knowledge of our Lord and Saviour Jesus Christ' (3:18) – bringing us back to where he started in 1:2–3.

Does this mean there's no progress? Clearly not. Verse 5 is an exhortation to make progress. The point is that we make progress in the Christian life by staying where we are! We make progress by remembering what we already know.

Why should I tell my wife 'I love you'? After all, I've told her before. It's not new information. Yet she loves to hear me say those words. She's never once said, 'You've already told me that. Please don't waste my time by telling me again.' She loves to hear those words because they reassure her of my love. They enable her to feel secure in our relationship. It's one area of her life in which she definitely doesn't want novelty! In the same way, the bride of Christ needs to hear him say, 'I love you.' And that's what he does say through the great and precious promises of the Bible. And the bride of Christ never grows tired of hearing those words. They reassure her, comfort her, give her security. They enable her to risk all to love him in return. They make her life productive and effective.

The Bible and the Spirit

So the Bible is both sufficient and necessary. We need the Bible to grow, and we only need the Bible. We can nuance this a little, because, of course, we also need God's help. We need the Holy Spirit to drive the word home in our hearts: to illuminate our minds, capture our affections and empower our wills. God always works through his word and his Spirit. And that means we need to pray. We need to pray as if we depend on God's help – because we do! But the point is this: we can't control the Spirit. The Spirit is not a tool I can pick up and use when I choose. As Jesus says, 'The wind blows wherever it pleases. You hear its sound, but you cannot tell where it comes from or where it is going. So it is with everyone born of the Spirit' (John 3:8).

So in terms of what I need for the job of 'life and godliness', it's the Bible to which I must turn. The Bible is the part of the task that I can do. A sailor can't switch on the wind or change its direction to suit his purposes. But a sailor can hoist the sail. In the same way, I can't switch on the Spirit or make him do what I want. But I can hoist the sail by exposing myself to God's word so that I catch the breath of the Spirit. I can read the Bible, hear it taught, encourage others with its teaching and look for people who will encourage me. I can make sure I don't forget the great and precious promises it contains.

Enough and more

'Have we brought enough food?' The word 'enough' can have the sense of the bare minimum. We scrape by with enough. But when we say the Bible is enough, we're saying something a bit more like, 'Enough! I couldn't possibly eat any more.' The Bible is not meagre rations, enough to get us through the day. The Bible is a feast that satisfies us deeply if only we would sit down intent on enjoying ourselves.

Or think of the Bible as a toolbox. Let's consider what it can do. What does it equip the servants of God to do? In 2 Timothy 3:16–17 it says, 'All Scripture is God-breathed and is useful for teaching, rebuking, correcting and training in righteousness, so that the servant of God may be thoroughly equipped for every good work.' Here's a tool that does the job. It teaches, rebukes, corrects and trains. It doesn't just equip; it *thoroughly* equips.

The value of the Bible to us is not that it's safely there on the shelf ready for when we need it. Yes, you can turn to it when you have a question or need help with a problem. But better still is to let it equip you. The blessing of the Bible comes when we so immerse ourselves in it that our spiritual blood becomes 'bibline', pumping God's precious promises to our souls. 'Cut me and I'll bleed the Bible,' we should be able to say.

As a pastor, I've noticed again and again that prevention is better than cure. People immersed in God's word respond better to life's problems. If people are not well rooted in God's word, it's difficult to bring that word to bear in a crisis. The truth that God works all things for our good, for example, can sound hard or harsh in the midst of heartbreak. But to people who already have a firm grasp of God's providence, its message proves a great comfort. That stability comes as your blood becomes 'bibline'.

8

The Bible is reliable

The Bible, says Peter, is 'completely reliable' (2 Peter 1:19). In the previous chapter we saw how Peter says God's word is enough. It gives us all we need for a godly life. That's a big claim. But can the Bible be trusted? Will it deliver? Is it true? Is it all true? Peter anticipates these questions and answers with a big 'Yes'.

The apostolic testimony

> For we did not follow cleverly devised stories when we told you about the coming of our Lord Jesus Christ in power, but we were eyewitnesses of his majesty. He received honour and glory from God the Father when the voice came to him from the Majestic Glory, saying, 'This is my Son, whom I love; with him I am well pleased.' We ourselves heard this voice that came from heaven when we were with him on the sacred mountain.
>
> (2 Peter 1:16–18)

Liberal Christianity claims that the Bible contains 'myths'. The miracle stories shouldn't be taken literally, we're told. They're 'myths' – stories created to embody spiritual truths. So we should take them 'seriously', but not as historical facts.

It sounds plausible and it certainly looks like it might help persuade our sceptical friends. And the Bible clearly does contain invented stories designed to communicate the truth – parables are a clear example. But what the Bible presents as historical events were not made up. They did happen. Peter explicitly says, 'we did not follow cleverly devised myths' (verse 16, ESV). Indeed, in the New Testament the word 'myth' is never used to describe a way of embodying truth. It's always the opposite of truth (1 Timothy 1:4; 4:7; 2 Timothy 4:4; Titus 1:14). Christianity is not a set of timeless religious insights or ethical principles. It's tied to events in history. Historical facts mattered to the writers of the New Testament. Thomas refused to believe the resurrection until he had evidence (John 20:25). Luke had 'carefully investigated' the historical facts before writing his Gospel (Luke 1:3). And Peter emphasizes that the apostles were 'eyewitnesses'. They saw the life, death and resurrection of Jesus for themselves. Modern scholars are very smart people. But Peter was there in Capernaum, by Lake Galilee (and on Lake Galilee at one point), in the Jerusalem temple. He hung around during the trial of Jesus. He saw Jesus die, entered the empty tomb and ate breakfast with the risen Christ. These were not gullible people ready to believe anything they were told. Nor were they inclined to exaggerate or elaborate. They were eyewitnesses who gave their lives for what they witnessed.

Peter singles out one particular event, the transfiguration. There are, I think, a number of reasons for this. First, what Peter witnessed was not just the remarkable acts of a man. He witnessed the 'majesty' of the Son of God affirmed by the voice of God the Father. The 'majesty' of Jesus in verse 16 is matched by the 'Majestic Glory' in verse 17. The 'glory' Jesus receives comes from the 'Majestic Glory'. Jesus the Son of God is as majestic and glorious as the Father.

Second, on the mountain Jesus appeared with Moses and Elijah. Together they represent 'the prophetic word' that Peter will go on to talk about in verses 19–21. Peter also adds that this took place 'on the sacred mountain'. The implication is that the transfiguration parallels the encounter with God at Mount Sinai when he gave the law. So Peter is lining up the apostolic testimony alongside the Law and the Prophets. The revelation of God in Christ proclaimed by the apostles is up there with the Old Testament Scriptures. The New Testament is Scripture just like the Old Testament.

Third, the transfiguration confirms two disputed events. The voice from heaven says, 'This is my Son, whom I love. Listen to him!' (Mark 9:7). We might expect the voice to say, '*Look* upon him', since Jesus is 'dazzling white' (Mark 9:3). So why say, 'Listen to him'? The answer is that Peter has just *refused to listen* to Jesus. In Mark 8:31–32, Peter rebukes Jesus when Jesus predicts his death for the first time. So the voice from heaven is confirming what Jesus says about the necessity of the cross. For Jews the cross was a curse; for Greeks it was folly. But the transfiguration is God's confirmation that the cross is his power for salvation.

The transfiguration also took place six days after Jesus had said, 'Truly I tell you, some who are standing here will not taste death before they see that the kingdom of God has come with power' (Mark 9:1). So it seems that the transfiguration was an anticipation of the future glory of Jesus. That's significant because the return of Christ is what's being disputed among Peter's readers, as we discover in 2 Peter 3. So Peter is saying that not only are the apostles eyewitnesses of the past, they're also eyewitnesses of the future. The future promises of the Bible are confirmed by the foretaste they received on the mountain.

So the New Testament is reliable because it's based on the Spirit-enabled eyewitness testimony of the apostles.

The prophetic word

But what about the Old Testament? Can we trust the Old Testament? That's the question to which Peter now turns:

> We also have the prophetic message as something completely reliable, and you will do well to pay attention to it, as to a light shining in a dark place, until the day dawns and the morning star rises in your hearts. Above all, you must understand that no prophecy of Scripture came about by the prophet's own interpretation of things. For prophecy never had its origin in the human will, but prophets, though human, spoke from God as they were carried along by the Holy Spirit.
> (2 Peter 1:19–21)

As we've noted already, there are people who say that the Bible records acts of divine revelation, but that the Bible itself is not an act of revelation. God revealed himself through the exodus, appeared on Mount Sinai, spoke to the prophets. And what we have in the Bible is an interpretation of those acts of revelation. It gives us enough to go on, but it's not always entirely accurate. It feels like a good compromise. We can make some doctrinal affirmations without having to defend everything the Bible says.

But again, this is not what Peter says. The Scriptures are not simply 'the prophet's own interpretation of things'. It's not the product of a human decision. Yes, there were human authors, and their distinctive personalities are reflected in what they wrote. But the Bible is 'from God'. The human authors 'were carried along by the Holy Spirit'.

Notice, too, that Peter speaks of the 'prophecy of Scripture'. It's literally 'the prophetic writings'. What's inspired is not just the prophetic message, but also the prophetic *writings*. God specifically told Jeremiah to 'write in a book all the words I have spoken to you' (Jeremiah 30:2). God is interested not just in the original proclamation of the prophets, but in the enduring record of that message.

What Peter literally says in verse 19 is that we have 'the prophetic word made more firm'. The Old Testament was already firm. But now it's been confirmed or firmed up by its fulfilment in Christ. If I told you I'd take you out for a meal, then your confidence in my promise would depend on your confidence in me. Let's suppose, just for the sake of argument, that you're confident I can and will deliver. Then you would regard that as a firm promise. If I then do indeed buy you a meal, that would confirm the promise. Firm and more firm. In the same way, the Old Testament promises were firm because they were made by God, and we can trust him to deliver. Now they're more firm because God *has* delivered in the person of his Son. In Isaiah 41:21–29, God says the test of a true God and true Scriptures is that they're able to predict the future. Peter says the Old Testament has passed this test.

So the Bible is a divine act. What's at stake is not so much the trustworthiness of the Bible as the trustworthiness of God. The Bible is not an account of religious experience or religious aspiration. It's not the product of scholarly studies or monastic contemplation. It's a message from God. And God can be trusted.

Some Christians believe the Bible is infallible, by which they mean it's true in all that it intends to do. They believe what it says about God and the key historical events of salvation is all true. But they allow for the possibility that incidental details may be inaccurate, since they're not part of God's intent in the Bible. Other Christians believe that the Bible is inerrant, by which they mean it contains no errors at all. All its historical details are accurate. Inerrancy is rooted in the Trinity: God the Father reveals himself in the Bible, and God is all-knowing and he does not lie. God the Son is the revelation recorded in the Bible, and he is the Truth. God the Spirit ensures that the record of the revelation of the Son is accurate. This view of the Bible is confirmed by Jesus. Jesus always treats the Old Testament as a word from God and an utterly reliable word.

It's important to recognize what inerrancy does not require. It does not require that we take everything literally. It allows for the normal conventions of speech and literature:

- Many numbers are approximated or rounded. If I tell my wife a book cost £10 when the price tag says £9.99, is that an error? No, we don't expect such precision in ordinary conversation. Arguably, it conveys more truth since £9.99 is intended to make us think the cost is around £9.[1]
- The writers weren't writing according to the standards of modern science. We don't expect that of most writers today (unless they're writing for scientific journals), and we shouldn't expect it of biblical writers.
- Speeches and reported speech are summarized.
- The literary conventions of the day are used, such as missing out generations in lists (as Matthew does in Matthew 1) or calling grandfathers 'fathers'.
- Quotes from other parts of the Bible are often cited freely.

- The writers sometimes arranged their material thematically, so events are not in chronological sequence – something often done by biographers today without anyone accusing them of inaccuracy.
- Irony, questions, vows, jokes, exclamations, hyperbole and greetings are all used, which are not true in the same way that statements are true.
- The fact that the Bible says something does not necessarily mean it receives divine endorsement. Ecclesiastes says, 'Everything is meaningless', but this is only true when you look at life 'under the sun' apart from God.
- Figures of speech are used.

Psalm 19:6 says the sun rises. It's a poetic image. We understand what it means without concluding that the sun revolves round the earth. People today use this kind of language in everyday speech. Your newspaper will give a time for 'sunset'. Of course, the sun rising in Psalm 19 is an easy example. With some parts of Scripture it's less obvious whether they should be taken literally or figuratively. Some people who believe in inerrancy think Genesis 1 is a poetic account of creation, while others take it literally.

All these factors don't undermine the authority of the Bible. They don't involve any attempt to mislead the reader. They're simply part of the way it communicates its message.

What about the contradictions in the Bible?

'What about all the discrepancies in the Bible?' This line is frequently used to dismiss biblical authority. Often the questioner is hard-pressed to list any actual discrepancies, and it's simply a convenient way to avoid the implications of the gospel. Nevertheless, there are apparent discrepancies, and we must address them honestly and openly.

Some discrepancies are inconsistencies with the findings of archaeology. But pots don't talk. In other words, archaeological findings require interpretation. And all those interpretations reflect presuppositions. Plus every interpretation is provisional and susceptible to new discoveries. There's plenty of archaeological evidence that supports the Bible's accounts. But in other areas the situation remains ambiguous. There's still little archaeological evidence for (or against) the exodus, for example.

Some discrepancies involve apparent contradictions within the Bible. Did Jesus open the eyes of two blind men as he was leaving Jericho (Matthew 20:29–30), or one blind man as he was leaving (Mark 10:46), or one blind man as he was entering the city (Luke 18:35)?

Many of these contradictions are easily accounted for. For others we can give plausible accounts, even if we're not sure which is the correct explanation. Some are the writer's way of getting us to think more deeply. See, for example, Proverbs 26:4–5; John 13:36 and 16:5; 9:39 and 12:47; 7:28 and 8:14. Charles Dickens begins *A Tale of Two Cities*, 'It was the best of times; it was the worst of times.' Is that an invitation to reflect on different perspectives or a contradiction that ruins the book?

Here are some options for the Jericho question:

- Jesus healed two men, but Mark and Luke focus on one.
- Jesus healed one when he entered the city and two more when he left.
- Jesus left the city, met Zacchaeus and then returned with Zacchaeus to his house, so his 'leaving' also became his 'entering'.

- Jesus met them on his way into the city and healed them on his way out.
- There was an old and a new city, and Jesus healed between the two.

Which, if any, is correct? I have no idea. I wasn't there at the time. But I'm confident there is an explanation.

What about the contradictions with our modern world?

Some discrepancies involve sharp contradictions with our cultural norms. People find the Bible's teaching on sexuality, gender, slavery, religious pluralism and judgment offensive. Each of these topics merits a book in its own right. They're important issues and can't be covered with a sound bite. We do, however, need to recognize that our culture is not a firm foundation from which to critique the Bible. You need only look at the fashions on show in old family photos to see that what our culture thinks is normative constantly changes. 'It should strike us as improbable, to say the least, that our twenty-first-century values should turn out to be the climax of humanity's moral journey.'[2]

But more importantly, if God is God, then we would expect him to confront our views at some point or other. The Bible is 'reassuringly unfashionable'.[3] Alluding to the film *The Stepford Wives* in which all the women of a town are alarmingly compliant, Tim Keller puts it like this:

> Now what happens if you eliminate anything from the Bible that offends your sensibility and crosses your will? If you pick and choose what you want to believe and reject the rest, how will you ever have a God who can contradict you? You won't! You'll have a Stepford God. A God, essentially, of your own

making, and not a God with whom you can have a relationship and genuine interaction. Only if your God can say things that can outrage you and make you struggle (as in a real friendship or marriage) will you know that you have got hold of a real God and not a figment of your imagination. So an authoritative Bible is not the enemy of a personal relationship with God. It is a precondition for it.[4]

The key question in these discussions is this: Who decides? Who's the judge? Who's the arbiter of truth? Are you going to assume you know better than God? 'The Christian revelation is a matter of gracious disclosure, not of human enquiry, and as a "word from God" it cannot be subject to human interrogation.'[5]

Have we got the right books in our Bible?

Which books belong in the Bible, and have we got the right ones? The collection of books in the Bible is called 'the canon'. According to Dan Brown's best-seller novel, *The Da Vinci Code*, the canon of Scripture was forced on the church at the Council of Nicea by the Emperor Constantine. In fact, the Council of Nicea didn't discuss the canon, and the Emperor also had nothing to do with it. But there is a less ridiculous version of this kind of claim which says that the church decided what was in the Bible and arbitrarily left out alternative perspectives so that the Bible ended up being an all-too-human construction.

In response, we need to realize that the canon of Scripture is not merely an anthology of Jewish and early Christian writings. What makes a book canonical is God. A book made it into the canon because it was authored by God and centred on his revelation in Christ. The first chapter of 2 Peter with its focus on the apostolic testimony and the prophetic writings gives us in embryonic form the basis by which this was determined. The Old Testament books were included because they contained the prophetic promise of Christ, while the New Testament books were included because they contained the apostolic testimony of Christ. So the church didn't arbitrarily decide what to include. It *recognized* which books were apostolic. The canon is based on Christ.

The Old Testament books in our Bibles are in a different order from those in the Jewish Scriptures. They follow the order of the Septuagint, the Greek translation of the Old Testament from the third century BC, probably because this was more accessible to most early Christians. But what's striking is that the early church didn't join the Septuagint in including the apocryphal books written after Malachi and the end of prophecy. Jude 14–15 quotes the extra-biblical 1 Enoch just as Paul quotes pagan sources (Acts 17:28; Titus 1:12). But the New Testament writers never quote apocryphal books as authoritative Scripture – despite attributing Old Testament quotes to God many, many times. They clearly saw the thirty-nine books of our Old Testament as in a different category from other writings – including the apocryphal books recognized by the Catholic Church. In Luke 11:50–51 Jesus says, 'This generation will be held responsible for the blood of all the prophets that has been shed since the beginning of the world, from the blood of Abel to the blood of Zechariah.' Why mention Abel and Zechariah? It's because in the order of books in the Hebrew Bible – which begins with Genesis and ends with Chronicles – they represent the first and last martyred prophets (Genesis 4:10; 2 Chronicles 24:21). The point for our purposes is that Jesus saw 2 Chronicles as the last book in the Bible, thereby excluding all the later apocryphal books. Jesus affirmed the Law, the Writings and the

Prophets of the Old Testament as Scripture, but not other books such as the apocryphal books.

All the New Testament books were connected to the apostolic testimony of Christ. They were written either by apostles or by people closely connected with an apostle (Mark was an associate of Peter, and Luke of Paul). In 2 Peter 3:16 it implies that, even in the apostolic period, the writings of Paul were part of the Scriptures. *The Da Vinci Code* claims that the church censored books like *The Gospel of Thomas*. But these books lacked credibility. They weren't omitted because the church didn't like them. Rather, they were omitted because they lacked the link to Christ.

God in his providence has preserved the Bible. For the first 1,500 years, copies of the Bible were all written out by hand. Inevitably, people made mistakes as they wrote. But God has ensured that we have reliable versions. We have hundreds of copies of the New Testament – far more than other works of ancient literature. Textual criticism is the discipline of taking all the hundreds of old Bible manuscripts and frag-ments to work out what the original must have been. There aren't many occasions when we can't be confident what the original was, and none of these involves significant doctrinal issues.

We trust what is trustworthy

Why do you trust the Bible? A strange thing can happen when we're faced by hostile questions from unbelievers. We forget all about why we believe the truth, and suddenly think we need some clever intellectual answer. In the case of the Bible, we start reading books about manuscript evidence, historical sources and archaeological findings. But let me ask my question again: Why do *you* trust the Bible? Perhaps you did undertake a thorough examination of the historical evidence. If so, good for you. But most of us trust because . . . well, we find it trustworthy. Manuscript evidence and archaeological findings may support our confidence in the Bible. But like our relationship with people, most of us find the Bible reliable because it has proved to be reliable in our lives.

Why do I trust my wife? Is it because I have her tailed by a private detective, checking that she's never unfaithful to me? No, I trust my wife because I've found her ever and always to be trustworthy.

And so it is with the Bible. We worry about how we might respond to questions about inconsistencies in the Bible or the evidence for evolution. But few of us needed these questions resolved before we believed. We initially believed and continue to believe because we find in the Bible words of life, comfort and hope. We believe the Bible because it makes sense of life. As C. S. Lewis famously said, 'I believe in Christianity as I believe that the Sun has risen, not only because I see it, but because by it I see everything else.'[6]

We've seen how 2 Peter 1 affirms that the Bible is from God. 'Prove it,' you might be saying. But Peter has embedded the key evidence in what he says. He says that the New Testament apostles were eyewitnesses 'of his majesty' (verse 16), and that the Old Testament is 'a light shining in a dark place, until the day dawns and the morning star rises in your hearts' (verse 19). The proof of the Bible's divine origins is that it displays the majesty of Christ and shines with the light of the gospel.

The taste test

My wife is a big fan of the television show *The Great British Bake Off*. At the climax of each episode, cakes baked by the contestants are brought to the front to be judged. We at home can all see the cakes. But none of us can tell which is a great cake. The only real way to know is the taste test. So Mary Berry puts a fork-full in her mouth, pauses, smiles and says, 'That's lovely.'

The true test of whether the Bible is God's word is the taste test. In 1 Peter 1:23 it says we've been 'born again . . . through the living and enduring word of God'. He then applies this truth. 'Like newborn babies, crave pure spiritual milk, so that by it you may grow up in your salvation' (2:2). The word that gave us birth is the word that makes us grow. Then he adds, '. . . now that you have tasted that the Lord is good' (2:3). We know the Bible is 'the living and enduring word of God' because in it and through it we 'have tasted that the Lord is good'.

The real deal

My daughter is an art historian. When she was little, her mother and I used to drag her round art galleries. Now she drags us round. A few years ago we visited the Musée d'Orsay in Paris. It's the home to several paintings by Vincent van Gogh. And oh my word, it's quite something to see his paintings in real life. Like the work of no other painter I know, the real thing is so much better than any reproduction. The paint shines out from the canvas. It's mesmerizing. When you see a van Gogh, you know it's the real deal.

In a similar way, when the word of God was preached to us, God 'made his light shine in our hearts to give us the light of the knowledge of God's glory displayed in the face of Christ' (2 Corinthians 4:6). We know the Bible is the real deal because in it we see the glory of Christ. His glory shines out from its pages.

It's important to realize how this works. It's not that the Bible is 'true for me' in a subjective sense. This is not simply an argument from experience – although experience is involved. I'm confident that van Gogh is a great painter because I've seen his paintings. But I didn't make them great. I merely recognized greatness when I saw it. In the same way, the taste test doesn't make Scripture good. It was good all along. All I did was recognize it as good when I tasted it.

This explains why people don't have to read the whole Bible before deciding to trust it. You don't need to eat the whole cake to know it's a great cake. Seeing the glory of Christ in the pages of the Bible sets you up to make the effort to explore its more obscure regions. I was once asked whether I'd read all the texts of all the world's religions. I hadn't. And truth be told, I've still not got round to it. 'How then,' asked my friend, 'can you know Christianity is the true one?' But that's like asking a newly engaged man, 'How can you know she's the one for you until you've been out with every woman in the world?' You'd get short shrift (I hope). Once you've met the real deal, your search is over.

The theological term for this is 'self-authenticating'. The Bible is 'self-authenticating'. When you see the glory of Christ in its pages, you know it's the real deal.

The great seventeenth-century English theologian John Owen speaks of the 'self-evidencing efficacy of the Scripture'. He uses the illustration of light. 'Light manifests light,' he says. 'Let the least child bring a candle into a room that before was dark, and it would be madness to go about to prove by substantial witnesses – men of gravity and authority – that light is brought in.' In the same way, 'the Scripture, the Word of God, is light . . . It is a light so shining with the majesty of its Author, as that it manifests itself to be his.' The word 'hath in itself a sufficiency of light to evidence to all'.[7] So the authority of Scripture comes from God himself:

> Now, this light in the Scripture, for which we contend, is
> nothing but the beaming of the majesty, truth, holiness, and
> authority of God, given unto it and left upon it by its authority,
> the Holy Ghost – an impress it hath of God's excellency upon
> it, distinguishing it by infallible signs from the product of any
> creature. By this it dives into the consciences of men, into all
> the secret recesses of their hearts; guides, teaches, directs,
> determines, and judges *in* them, *upon* them, in the name,
> majesty, and authority of God.[8]

As Owen acknowledges, not everyone recognizes this. Plenty of people have read the Bible and found it tasted repugnant to them. The reason, Paul explains, is, 'The god of this age has blinded the minds of unbelievers, so that they cannot see the light of the gospel that displays the glory of Christ' (2 Corinthians 4:4). This means trusting the Bible is the work of the Holy Spirit. The Spirit opens our blind eyes to see the glory of Christ in the pages of the Bible. Our job is humbly to immerse ourselves in the Bible while praying for the illumination of the Spirit. Here's how Question 4 of the Westminster Larger Catechism puts it:

> The Scriptures manifest themselves to be the Word of God,
> by their majesty and purity; by the consent of all the parts,
> and the scope of the whole, which is to give all glory to God;
> by their light and power to convince and convert sinners,
> to comfort and build up believers unto salvation: but the
> Spirit of God bearing witness by and with the Scriptures
> in the heart of man, is alone able fully to persuade it that
> they are the very word of God.

Again, the trinitarian nature of Scripture is key. How do I know the Bible is reliable? Because I see in it the glory of Christ as the Spirit opens my blind eyes.

This also brings us back to the central theme of this book. The reason why we trust the Bible is that in it and through it we have heard God's voice and encountered his presence.

Psalm 29 opens with an exhortation to 'ascribe to the LORD the glory due to his name' and to 'worship the LORD in the splendour of his holiness' (verse 2). It then switches focus from the glory of the LORD to 'the voice of the LORD': 'The voice of the LORD is powerful' and 'majestic'. It breaks the cedars, strikes with lightning, shakes the desert, twists the oaks. And then we read, 'And in his temple all cry, "Glory!"' When the people of God hear the voice of God in his word, we cry 'Glory'. We recognize it when we see it (or read it) and instinctively cry out in worship. The voice of God inevitably brings us back to the glory of God. We see in his word 'the splendour of his holiness'.

Charles H. Spurgeon was famously fond of saying that he would rather defend a lion than defend the Bible. His point was the Bible doesn't need us to defend it. It is, as we've seen, powerful and active. The best way to defend it is to expose people to it. Suppose someone asks you why you believe the Bible when it's 2,000-plus years old, full of contradictions and homophobic. Invite them to read it with you. Here's how Spurgeon put it:

> I believe the best way of defending the Gospel is to spread the Gospel! . . . Suppose a number of persons were to take it into their heads that they had to defend a lion, a full-grown king of beasts! There he is in a cage and here come all the soldiers of the army to fight for him. Well, I would suggest to them, if they would not object and feel that it was humbling

to them, that they should kindly stand back, open the door, and let the lion out![9]

I don't have to prove my sword is genuine before I thrust it into an opponent. It will still work whether he believes in it or not. The Bible is the sword of the Spirit (Ephesians 6:17). We can wield it with confidence without waiting for people to believe in it. Then we may find that it's 'sharper than any double-edged sword'. We may find that 'it penetrates even to dividing soul and spirit, joints and marrow' and that 'it judges the thoughts and attitudes of the heart' (Hebrews 4:12).

9

The Bible is accessible

Secret messages have been encoded in the Hebrew text of the Bible. If you start with a letter and then repeatedly count on by the fixed number, then hidden phrases begin to appear. These correctly predicted the 1995 assassination of Yitzhak Rabin, the Israeli Prime Minister. Such are the claims of Michael Drosnin in his bestselling book, *The Bible Code*.

It is, of course, rubbish. The encoded messages turn out to be extremely vague, and Drosnin's predictions have proved to be wrong. If you start with enough different letters and skip by enough different intervals, then you'll get some kind of message in any document.

Drosnin is an extreme example. But plenty of people claim to find secret messages or allusions to specific contemporary events in the text of Scripture.

But the Bible is not written in code. It's clear and understandable. You don't need someone to unlock its meaning for you. In medieval Catholicism the meaning of Scripture was the preserve of the church hierarchy. You needed a priest to tell you what Scripture said. Indeed, the church was suspicious of letting ordinary people read the Bible for fear they might misinterpret it. In liberal Protestantism it's the scholar who tells you the meaning of Scripture. The scholar has become the new pope, as it were. Only an expert can tell us what it really means, we're told.

But this not what the Bible itself says. Psalm 119:130 says, 'The unfolding of your words gives light; it gives understanding to the simple.' This doesn't mean the Bible is always easy to understand (as Peter acknowledges in 2 Peter 3:16). So the early Church Fathers and the Reformers all emphasized that we understand the obscure parts of the Bible in the light of the clear parts. We use Scripture to interpret Scripture. Neither does it mean that the Bible answers every question we have. It doesn't even answer every question about God. Deuteronomy 29:29 says, 'The secret things belong to the LORD our God, but the things revealed belong to us and to our children for ever, that we may follow all the words of this law.' But the Bible is clear on everything we need to know in order to follow God.

Nor does this mean we don't need Bible teachers and preachers. On the road to Gaza, Philip met an Ethiopian eunuch who was reading from Isaiah. 'Do you understand what you are reading?' Philip asked. 'How can I,' he said, 'unless someone explains it to me?' (Acts 8:30–31). If Scripture interprets Scripture, then it helps to have people gifted by the Spirit who know the Scriptures well. But every good Bible teacher invites his hearers to judge what he says in the light of Scripture.

The point is the Bible is not written in code, nor does it have to be mediated through an elite – whether that's a priest or a scholar. Its message doesn't need to be validated by human institutions. The Westminster Confession of Faith puts it like this:

All things in Scripture are not alike plain in themselves, nor
alike clear unto all: yet those things which are necessary to
be known, believed, and observed for salvation are so clearly
propounded, and opened in some place of Scripture or other,
that not only the learned, but the unlearned, in a due use
of the ordinary means, may attain unto a sufficient
understanding of them.[1]

Desiderius Erasmus was Europe's leading celebrity academic
in the sixteenth century. In 1524 he was persuaded to publish
an attack on Martin Luther and the Reformation. The issue
at stake was whether human beings have the capacity to please
God. But Erasmus begins by talking about Scripture. 'I confess
it is right,' he says, 'that the sole authority of Holy Scripture
should outweigh all the votes of all mortal men.' So far so
good. But he continues, 'The authority of the Scripture is
not here in dispute . . . Our battle is about the meaning of
Scripture.'[2] He goes on to say that we need the authority
of the Church to determine the true meaning of Scripture.
The reason is what he calls the 'obscurity in Scripture'. When
faced with different interpretations, we should remember that
'God has infused his Spirit into those whom he has ordained.'[3]
In other words, we should submit to the pope. 'Moreover,
some things there are of such a kind that, even if they were
true and might be known, it would not be proper to prostitute
them before common ears.'[4] So there you go. According to
Erasmus, some Bible truths are too sophisticated for the likes
of you and me!

In response, Luther says, 'The subject matter of the
Scriptures . . . is all quite accessible, even though some texts
are still obscure owing to our ignorance.'[5] Luther points to
the many times in the Bible where the writers assume the
word of God can be understood. He refers to 2 Timothy 3:16:

'All Scripture is God-breathed and is useful for teaching, rebuking, correcting and training in righteousness.' Using humour, he says that if Erasmus is right, then we should say, 'Nay, Paul, it is not profitable at all, but the things you attribute to Scripture must be sought from the Fathers who have been approved for hundreds of years, and from the Roman See!'[6]

Luther speaks of two kinds of clarity. There's an internal clarity that only comes when the Spirit enlightens our darkened hearts. It's the spiritual blindness that this cures which explains why many people misunderstand the Bible. But there's also an external clarity. 'Nothing at all is left obscure or ambiguous, but everything there is in the Scriptures has been brought out by the Word into the most definite light, and published to all the world.'[7] What makes God's word clear is both the Bible and the Spirit. We hear God's voice clearly because it's clearly recorded in the Bible *and* because the Spirit frees us from the blindness of self-will and self-justification. So the Bible is simple enough for a child to understand, yet hides its truth from the proud (Luke 10:21; 1 Corinthians 3:18–20).

Here's the key point. Luther says, 'If Scripture is obscure or ambiguous, what point was there in God giving it to us?'[8] It brings us back to our central theme. The Bible is given to us by God with intent. And for it to achieve that intent, its overall message must be clear. It's not written in code, nor in such sophisticated language that only an elite can understand it. The clarity of Scripture is ultimately rooted in God himself and his saving purposes. God wrote the Bible to communicate and so it communicates clearly. Mark Thompson says,

> The clarity of Scripture needs to be placed firmly in the context of the living God's involvement with the world

he has made and the people he has redeemed. It needs explicit relation to the character of God and his saving activity, in particular his determination to be known by men and women in and through the person of Jesus Christ. On such terms an exposition of the clarity of Scripture becomes a confession of faith in the benevolence of our heavenly Father, a confession anchored in the redemptive work of the Son and made possible in the present by the operation of the Holy Spirit on sinful human hearts and otherwise suspicious human minds.[9]

Is the Bible really clear?

One objection to the clarity of the Bible is this: 'God is so transcendent that we can't nail him down to one interpretation. It's arrogant to claim to know *the* truth about God. At best, we can have different perceptions.' There's some truth in this. God can't easily be nailed down. He's beyond our comprehension. But the Bible is not a record of human religious experience or attempts to express religious truth. It's God himself who speaks in the Bible, and he speaks to communicate. While we can't understand God *fully* because he's transcendent, we can understand him *truly* because he graciously communicates to us.

A second objection is this: 'If the Bible is so clear, why are there so many different interpretations?' Again, it's true that some parts of the Bible are hard to understand and some theological ideas are controversial. But the main message of the Bible is clear. Luther says, 'If the words are obscure in one place, yet they are plain in another.'[10]

The answer to both these objections is the same. God himself speaks in the Bible. And he's not playing games with us. He has a purpose when he communicates and he is perfectly capable of making himself clear.

Imagine a mother telling her three daughters to go to bed. 'I think she's inviting us to go to bed if we want,' says one. 'I think she's expressing her own longing to go to bed and projecting that on to to us,' says another. The third says, 'I think bed is a symbol to convey the deep longing we all have for inner peace.' How is their mother going to respond? 'My intentions are perfectly clear, and if you don't do what I say, then you'll be in big trouble.' Language works. Of course, sometimes there are misunderstandings. But think about your own experience. Ninety-nine per cent of the time, what you say is understood without problem. And God's communication is no different. Some passages of the Bible are hard to understand. But the overall message is clear enough. The problems only really arise when, like the daughters, we don't like what we hear and so we twist what God says.

Making sense of the Bible

There are a few simple principles that help us read the Bible well. They're not arbitrary; they arise out of what we've already learnt about the nature of the Bible.

Principle #1. The Bible is intentional, so look for the author's intended meaning

In chapter 6 we saw that God intends to speak through his word to establish a covenantal relationship with its hearers and readers. Reading the Bible needs to honour this. The meaning of the text is the meaning intended by the divine and human author. In chapter 6 we explored the way this shapes how we read the Bible.

Principle #2. God spoke Jesus in the Bible, so follow the story of God's promises to Jesus

In chapter 4 we saw that the central message that God communicates in the Bible is Jesus and his work. One way or another, all Scripture leads to Jesus. Jesus is the Word of God, the ultimate revelation of God. The Old Testament is the promise of his coming, and the New Testament is the record of his coming. Together they explain the significance of Jesus and his work for us. In chapter 4 we explored the way this shapes how we read the Bible.

Principle #3. God spoke using words, so texts make sense in context

In chapter 2 we saw that God spoke in the Bible. He chose to communicate using words through human authors. This means the normal rules of reading apply. God communicated in a way (writing) that already existed, with its conventions and norms. And he did this because it was an effective way of communicating. But it only communicates effectively if we follow those norms. In particular, texts make sense in context, and they reflect the style of literature in which they're written.

What would happen if you read a novel as you do an encyclopedia – dipping in and reading an isolated paragraph? The answer, of course, is that you wouldn't be able to make much sense of it. The Bible is much more like a novel than an encyclopedia. Verses or paragraphs read out of context won't make much sense. This is what the Swiss Reformer Huldrych Zwingli says of picking out verses without regard to their context:

It is like breaking off a flower from its roots and trying
to plant it in a garden. But that is not the way: you must

plant it with the roots and the soil in which it is
embedded. And similarly we must leave the Word
of God its own proper nature if its sense is to be the
same to all of us.[11]

Consider the following statement: 'I'm mad about my car.'
The word 'mad' could mean enthusiastic or it could mean
angry. Taken on its own, the statement is unclear. But add a
bit of context and it becomes clearer: 'I'm mad about my car
because it was stolen from right outside my house.' Context
clarifies a text. It can even alter what we originally thought
it meant.

The sentence, 'I, when I am lifted up from the earth, will
draw all men to myself' in John 12:32, on its own might easily
be understood to mean that when we lift Jesus up in our
evangelism or praise, people will be drawn to him. But, true
though that may be, it's not what Jesus meant when he said
these words. John explains what he meant in the next verse:
'He said this to show by what kind of death he was going
to die' (John 12:33). Jesus is talking about being lifted up on to
the cross. In John's Gospel the cross is portrayed as the
moment when Jesus is glorified. His lifting up to die is also his
lifting up in glory.

So texts only make sense in their context. This is true at all
levels. Looking at the text in its context involves looking at:

- sentences in the context of paragraphs;
- paragraphs in the context of sections;
- sections in the context of whole books;
- books in the context of the Bible story as a whole.

So a key question to ask yourself is always: What's the flow of
the passage? What's the logic of the argument? What does

each sentence and paragraph add? How do they elaborate, develop or apply what's already been said? Look for connecting words like 'for', 'therefore', 'but', 'if', 'since', 'for this reason', 'so that', 'because' and 'then', because they indicate the links between the different parts of an argument. I often pause in my deliberations to reread the passage to see if I can make sense of the flow. I want to be sure I know how it all fits together and how every part contributes to the argument. I don't simply want to know what a verse means. I want to know *why it's there*. I'll often do this several times as I work on a passage. I never want to lose sight of the big picture as I delve into the detail. Or, to put it the other way round, I want the detail to be constantly improving my understanding of the main argument.

Individual words also make sense in context. The same word can have different meanings. The word 'hope', for example, in our culture usually means a vague optimism. But in the New Testament it conveys the idea of certain expectation. The fact that an Old Testament prophet talks about 'Israel' doesn't mean he is referring to the modern State of Israel. He's speaking about the people of God in his day. Even within the Bible, the same word can have different meanings at different times and in different genres. So context is key. And the primary context of the New Testament is the Old Testament. So often New Testament words are shaped by the Old Testament story. For example, the word 'redemption' is frequently a shorthand term for the exodus from slavery in Egypt. So its use in the New Testament often conveys the idea of a new exodus from the slavery of sin through the Passover sacrifice of Jesus Christ. In the Bible the meanings of names are often significant, especially when the naming is part of the story, or an explanation of the name is given in the text.

The significance of words, ideas and events is in part shaped by the cultural and historical background in which they were first spoken. For example, it would have been seen as undignified for Middle Eastern patriarchs in the time of Jesus to run. If we know this, we detect an even greater significance in the actions of the father who runs to meet his prodigal son in Luke 15. Sometimes the text itself supplies us with a significant piece of cultural or historical information (John 4:9). Meanwhile, be cautious about cultural information from only one commentator or with no apparent foundation in primary sources. For example, it's sometimes said that 'the eye of the needle' (Mark 10:25) was a small gate in Jerusalem through which it was extremely difficult, but possible, to squeeze a camel. There's no evidence for this. One person's tentative suggestion can become someone else's confident assertion. People also sometimes wrongly assume the practices of one culture provide explanations of behaviour in another culture.

Principle #4. God spoke using words, so texts reflect their genre

Here are two accounts of the same event:

> Then Moses stretched out his hand over the sea, and all
> that night the LORD drove the sea back with a strong east
> wind and turned it into dry land. The waters were divided,
> and the Israelites went through the sea on dry ground,
> with a wall of water on their right and on their left.
> (Exodus 14:21–22)

> The waters saw you, God,
>   the waters saw you and writhed;
>   the very depths were convulsed.

The clouds poured down water,
  the heavens resounded with thunder;
  your arrows flashed back and forth.
Your thunder was heard in the whirlwind,
  your lightning lit up the world;
  the earth trembled and quaked.
Your path led through the sea,
  your way through the mighty waters,
  though your footprints were not seen.
You led your people like a flock
  by the hand of Moses and Aaron.
(Psalm 77:16–20)

Did the waters of the Red Sea have eyes, as Psalm 77 suggests? Of course not. This is figurative language. The Bible is written in different styles of literature or genres: stories, letters, poetry, wisdom, laws, parables, apocalyptic and so on. Each of these has its own conventions.

Narrative and letters involve more literal statements, while poetry and apocalyptic are full of imagery. Not that everything in letters is literal. In Philippians 2:17, for example, Paul talks about being 'poured out like a drink offering'. But he's not literally turning to liquid! Remember, 'figurative' is not the same as 'false'. Figurative statements express truth in non-literal ways in order to maximize the emotional impact.

Bible writers also often use hyperbole – deliberate exaggeration to make a point. For example, in Luke 14:26, Jesus talks about hating your parents. He doesn't expect us to take it literally. The point is that if there's a conflict of interests, then we should choose Jesus. But that doesn't mean we should 'tone down' hyperboles. Jesus is exaggerating in this way because we need to feel the force of the point being made.

Principle #5. God speaks in the Bible, so identify the implications for today

In chapter 3 we saw that God speaks in the present through the Holy Spirit, so the Bible is a contemporary word. In chapter 6 we saw that the Bible is intentional: God rules through his word. This means we can never read the Bible as disinterested observers. It implicates us. We're called to respond in faith and repentance. Reading the Bible results in either obedience or disobedience. It never results in nothing. So as we read, we need to identify the implications for us today.

We start by asking what response the original author wanted from his hearers or readers. Identifying the application *then* will take you ninety per cent of the way towards identifying the implications for us *now*. This may be an action to do. But it may also be confidence in truth, grief over sin, joy in Christ, compassion for others, praise to God, wonder at grace and so on. Application is not confined to explicit commands, but they can be good pointers. Is there a command to obey, an example to follow, a promise to comfort, a sin to confess, a warning to heed?

Is this passage for unbelievers or believers? Is this passage for individual Christians or the Christian community as a whole? Is this passage for a particular type of person (leaders, parents, men, women)? Be careful when applying a truth intended for one group to another group. Make sure you identify the underlying principles.

Some implications will be implicit. Believing lies about God, says Paul, leads to impure behaviour (Romans 1:24–25). Believing the truth sets us free (John 8:31–32). So explore the kinds of behaviours and emotions that will flow from confidence in the truths expressed in the passage as well as the behaviours that will flow from *not* trusting these truths. If, for example, I truly believe that God is my heavenly Father, then I'll face financial problems with peace (Luke 12:22–31). But if I'm not trusting God, then I'll fret.

We are told in 1 Corinthians 10:6 that Bible stories were given as examples for us to follow or avoid. But this isn't always straightforward:

- Daniel continues to pray to God even though the king outlaws prayer to anyone but himself (Daniel 6). Should we copy Daniel and obey God rather than people?
- David commits adultery with Bathsheba and then murders her husband to cover up his actions (2 Samuel 11). Should we copy David and commit adultery?
- As a boy, Samuel hears God speaking in the night and revealing the future (1 Samuel 3). Should we copy Samuel and expect God audibly to reveal the future?

In these cases, Daniel is clearly an example we should follow and David is an example we should avoid. Samuel's story is harder to judge.

So how do we apply stories? Our first two principles help. Principle #1 is 'The Bible is intentional, so look for the author's intended meaning.' Is there anything in the author's portrayal of the story that suggests it's an example to follow or a warning to avoid?

Principle #2 is 'God spoke Jesus in the Bible, so follow the story of God's promises to Jesus.' So think what the actions of the characters reveal about their faith in God's promises. Biblical ethics are always the ethics of faith. We don't earn God's approval by doing good things. Our actions should flow from faith in God. How do you see this in the story? This approach will help to avoid moralism. For example, the main problem with Abraham and Sarah having a child by Hagar is that they do this because they don't trust God's promise of a child and therefore take matters into their own hands (Genesis 16).

Remember, God is always the 'hero' of the story. So the central question is always: What does this story reveal about God? Think carefully about whom you identify with in the story. Don't assume you should identify with the hero. The Bible story is not primarily about us; it's about Jesus. He's the central character. Jesus' compassion is an example we should follow, but we should identify primarily with the crowds who need his help. This is how Jesus himself applies the feeding of the 5,000 in John 6:25–59.

Principle #6. The Bible is good news, so look for gospel motives
The Bible is not primarily a list of moral obligations (although it does, of course, have big implications for our morality). Primarily, the Bible is gospel or good news. It's the good news of the Father's love to us, the Son's work for us and the Spirit's power in us.

Human beings have an inbuilt tendency towards self-justification, which means we interpret moral commands as a way to earn approval from God and other people. If we only look in the Bible for what we *ought* to do, then we'll view right behaviour as an obligation. As a result, we'll either feel self-righteous or defeated, depending on how we're doing. Instead, we need to see right behaviour as the fruit of God's grace.

In the world around us, 'who we are' (our identity) is the result of 'what we do' (our activity). If you keep on winning, then you'll become a champion. If you pass your exams, then you'll be a graduate. If your children do well, then you'll be seen as a good parent. The gospel turns this upside down. In the gospel our identity is a gift that we receive from God. We don't earn it. We receive through faith. Our activity then flows out of this new identity.

The Bible consistently reflects this pattern. The commands of the Bible always flow from statements of what God has done or who we are in Christ. The Ten Commandments – the archetypal biblical commands – are introduced with these words: 'I am the LORD your God, who brought you out of Egypt, out of the land of slavery' (Exodus 20:2). God's activity leads to our identity, which leads to our activity.

Let's take an example. Colossians 3:12 says, 'Therefore, as God's chosen people, holy and dearly loved, clothe yourselves with compassion, kindness, humility, gentleness and patience.' It's easy for us to read this verse and think it's telling us to be compassionate, kind, humble, gentle and patient. And in one sense it is. But first and foremost, it's telling us that we're 'God's chosen people, holy and dearly loved'. Take a moment to think about that: you are *dearly loved* by God. That gives the command a very different feel. We're being asked to 'be what we are', to act as dearly loved people by loving one another. That's not all. The verse begins 'Therefore'. This command is the implication of what Paul has just been saying in verse 11, which is that in Christ social divisions don't matter any more. 'Christ is all, and is in all' (verse 11). Again, we're being asked to 'be what we are': a church united by Christ.

So as you read, look for:

- the statements of who we are out of which commands flow;
- the motives the Bible itself gives for right behaviour.

Our goal should be to discover afresh God's generous love over and over again so that our hearts are captivated by him and our lives are devoted to him.

- We need to see the *greatness* of God so we *trust* him.
- We need to see the *glory* of God so we *fear* him.
- We need to see the *goodness* of God so we *desire* him.
- We need to see the *grace* of God so we *rest* in him.

There's one more principle for reading the Bible. It flows out of the fact that the Bible is relational. And it's the most important principle, so it gets a chapter all to itself . . .

10

Dying to read the Bible

The most important thing you need to know in order to read the Bible well is something you will discover in *your baptism*. Let me explain. Romans 6:3–4 says,

> Don't you know that all of us who were baptised into Christ Jesus were baptised into his death? We were therefore buried with him through baptism into death in order that, just as Christ was raised from the dead through the glory of the Father, we too may live a new life.

Paul says that your baptism was, in effect, a funeral service. Becoming a Christian is much more radical than merely a change of opinion or even a change of allegiance. When you became a Christian, you died to your old life as part of the old humanity in Adam. And you were raised to a new life as part of a new humanity in Christ. Baptism embodies or enacts this. We're buried under the water and then rise out of the water to a new life. Our baptism is God's declaration to us that our old self has died and we've risen to a new life.

When Paul tells the story of his own conversion in Acts, he describes how he fell to the ground and the Lord Jesus told him to 'Get up' (Acts 22:7, 10; 26:14, 16). The word translated 'get up' is used elsewhere to describe the resurrection of Jesus (Luke 18:33; 24:7; John 20:9). What Paul realized was that his conversion was an enactment of every conversion. We fall to the ground so that we can be raised up to a new life. Saul was on his way to Damascus to persecute the church. And then he met Jesus. And the man who got up from the ground was not the same person who had fallen from his horse. Saul rose again as Paul. The persecutor rose again as the missionary. Saul-in-Adam rose again as Paul-in-Christ.

But it doesn't stop there. When you become a Christian, you experience death and resurrection. But death and resurrection then become the pattern of our lives. We are constantly, repeatedly dying and rising – dying to self and rising to Christ, experiencing death and experiencing life. Once you start looking for it, you'll find this pattern all over the New Testament.

We've seen how Paul says our baptism embodies our death and resurrection with Christ at conversion. But Paul then goes on to apply this to our lives now. Our old self used to be ruled by sin, but God killed off that old self through the death of Christ (Romans 6:6–7). And we've risen again in Christ to a new life in which we need not be controlled by sin (verses 7–8). So verse 11 says, 'In the same way, count yourselves dead to sin but alive to God in Christ Jesus.'

Let's look at another example. Colossians 3:1–5 says,

> Since, then, you have been raised with Christ, set your hearts on things above, where Christ is, seated at the right hand of God. Set your minds on things above, not on earthly things. For you died, and your life is now hidden with Christ in God.

When Christ, who is your life, appears, then you also will appear with him in glory.

Put to death, therefore, whatever belongs to your earthly nature: sexual immorality, impurity, lust, evil desires and greed, which is idolatry.

Verse 3 says, 'you died' with Christ (see also 2:20), and verse 1 says, 'you have been raised with Christ'. Those statements are in the past tense. That's what happened when you became a Christian. But that shapes our present experience. Verse 5 says that we're to 'put to death, therefore, whatever belongs to your earthly nature'. We can do this because we have resurrection life. That resurrection life is hidden, in the sense that we don't have resurrection bodies. But we do have resurrection power, and that empowers us to put sin to death. So death is a daily reality for Christians – death to self and death to sin. And new life is a daily reality for Christ. We're constantly being re-energized, reborn, remade, renewed. That's what Paul says a few verses later in Colossians 3:9–11:

Do not lie to each other, since you have taken off your old self with its practices and have put on the new self, which is being renewed in knowledge in the image of its Creator. Here there is no Gentile or Jew, circumcised or uncircumcised, barbarian, Scythian, slave or free, but Christ is all, and is in all.

Paul changes the metaphor, but the idea is the same. Instead of dying and rising, it's taking off and putting on. We take off the old self and put on the new self. The word 'self' is the word 'humanity'. That's why verse 11 talks about how 'here' in the new humanity (not just the new self) different races are united. The old humanity was created in God's image. Now the new humanity is being recreated in God's image (verse 10).

John Calvin said repentance has two parts to it: 'mortification' and 'vivification'.[1] The word 'mortification' means 'putting to death' (think of the English word 'mortuary', which describes a place where dead bodies are kept). And 'vivification' means 'receiving life' (think of the English word 'vivacious', which describes a lively attitude). So mortification means putting sin to death – saying 'no' to temptation and 'sorry' for sin. And vivification means turning to God to receive new life and walking in step with the Spirit.

If all this leaves your head spinning, focus on this thought. Every day we experience death as we die to sin and self. And every day we experience new life as we're renewed by God.

This dying is not just spiritual; it's actually physical as well. Every day we're getting older, decaying, moving closer to the physical death. If you don't feel the effects of that now, then you soon will! But every day we're also being renewed. It says in 2 Corinthians 4:16, 'Though outwardly we are wasting away, yet inwardly we are being renewed day by day.' Every day we experience death; every day we experience new life. The death and resurrection of Jesus have their fingerprints all over the Christian life. And that includes reading the Bible.

Death and resurrection are what the Bible does to us

The Bible brings death and life. That's true because when it is preached, some people reject its message and are therefore judged, while others accept its message and therefore receive eternal life. But it's also true in the experience of Christians. Consider Hebrews 4:12–13:

> For the word of God is alive and active. Sharper than any double-edged sword, it penetrates even to dividing soul and spirit, joints and marrow; it judges the thoughts and attitudes

of the heart. Nothing in all creation is hidden from God's sight. Everything is uncovered and laid bare before the eyes of him to whom we must give account.

What does the Bible do? It judges and it uncovers. As we hear the Bible read and preached, our sin is judged. Our hearts are exposed. Our secrets are uncovered. The Bible is like a sword finding its way through our armour. It penetrates deep into our lives and hearts. 'Thoughts and attitudes' of which we were unaware are brought to the surface. We are unmade, exposed, crushed.

But for Christians, this always leads to new life. God never wounds his people except to bring healing. Hosea 6:1–2 says,

Come, let us return to the LORD.
He has torn us to pieces
    but he will heal us;
he has injured us
    but he will bind up our wounds.
After two days he will revive us;
    on the third day he will restore us,
    that we may live in his presence.

So again and again the Bible speaks of the way it brings life. Citing Deuteronomy 8:3, Jesus said, 'Man shall not live on bread alone, but on every word that comes from the mouth of God.' Just as bread gives life to our physical bodies, so the Bible gives life to our souls. In 1 Peter 2:2–3 the Bible is also compared to physical food, but this time it speaks of it as milk: 'Like newborn babies, crave pure spiritual milk, so that by it you may grow up in your salvation, now that you have tasted that the Lord is good.' Think how babies crave milk. If they're hungry, then there are no social niceties – they scream for it.

You can't persuade them to be patient. That's because without milk they die. And that's how we're to crave God's word. You don't need to do the screaming. But you do need to have that kind of desperate urgency, because without God's word we die. Our souls wither away.

Or consider the words of Jesus in John 6:63: 'The Spirit gives life; the flesh counts for nothing. The words I have spoken to you – they are full of the Spirit and life.' The Bible is *full of life*.

This describes our experience. Many times we've come to the Bible and found ourselves exposed and challenged. But also there have been many times when we've come to the Bible and found ourselves renewed, energized, comforted, excited.

This should shape our expectations:

- The Bible brings death and then brings life.
- The Bible wounds and then heals.
- The Bible judges and then justifies.
- The Bible exposes and then clothes.
- The Bible crushes and then revives.
- The Bible unmakes and then remakes.
- The Bible unmasks us and then gives us a new identity.

So every day as you open your Bible and every week as you hear it preached, expect to be wounded, judged, unmade, exposed, crushed. And expect to be healed, justified, remade, clothed, revived. Expect to experience death and life.

Death and resurrection are how we come to the Bible

So death and resurrection shape our expectations of the Bible. But they should also shape how we approach the Bible.

The discipline of understanding the Bible aright is called 'hermeneutics'. It's worth reflecting on the Bible's own hermeneutical principles, that is, how the Bible thinks it should be read.[2] Here we meet a set of priorities that you don't tend to find in most manuals of biblical interpretation. We read principles like this:

> The fear of the LORD is the beginning of knowledge,
>   but fools despise wisdom and instruction.
> (Proverbs 1:7)

> These are the ones I look on with favour:
>   those who are humble and contrite in spirit,
>   and who tremble at my word.
> (Isaiah 66:2)

Here the key principles are fear, humility, contrition or repentance, and trembling. If you want to read the Bible well, you need to come to it *trembling*.

In 1522 the Reformer Huldrych Zwingli published *The Clarity and Certainty of the Word of God*, which includes a list of twelve hermeneutic rules. Again, they're not the kind of principles we get today. Instead, he focuses on prayer, mortification, strength from God, humility, despair and the pursuit of divine comfort and joy.

> I thought it might be good at this point to give some instruction in the way to come to a true understanding of the Word of God and to a personal experience of the fact that you are taught of God. For if we are not versed in Scripture, how are we to tell whether the priest who teaches us is expounding the pure truth unadulterated by his own sinful desires?

First, we must pray inwardly to God, that he will kill off
the old man who sets such great store by his own wisdom
and ability.

Second, when the old man is killed off and removed,
that God will graciously infill us, and in such measure that
we believe and trust only in him.

Third, when that is done we shall certainly be greatly
refreshed and comforted, and we must constantly repeat
the words of the prophet: Lord, God, strengthen that which
thou hast wrought in us. For 'let him that thinketh he
standeth take heed lest he fall,' as Paul says.

Fourth, the Word of God does not overlook anyone,
and least of all the greatest. For when God called Paul,
he said to Ananias: 'He is a chosen vessel unto me, to
bear my name before the princes and kings of the earth.'
Again, he says to the disciples (Matt. 10): 'And ye shall be
brought before governors and kings, that ye may testify
unto them concerning me.'

Fifth, it is the nature and property of the Word to humble
the high and mighty and to exalt the lowly. That was the
song of the Virgin Mary: 'He hath put down the mighty from
their seats, and exalted them of low degree.' And again, John
proclaimed concerning Christ (Luke 3): 'By him shall all the
hills be brought low, and the valleys filled, etc.'

Sixth, the Word of God always attracts and helps the poor,
comforting the comfortless and despairing, but opposing those
who trust in themselves, as Christ testifies.

Seventh, it does not seek its own advantage: for that
reason Christ commanded his disciples to take neither scrip
nor purse.

Eighth, it seeks only that God may be revealed to men,
that the obstinate may fear him and the lowly find comfort
in God. Those who preach in that manner are undoubtedly

144 OF DYING TO READ THE BIBLE

right. Those who cautiously beat about the bush for their own advantage, defending the teaching of man instead of holding and expounding the doctrine of God, are false prophets. Know them by their words. They make a fine outcry: The holy Fathers! Is it nothing that man can do? and the like. But for all their complaining they do not complain that the Gospel of Christ is slackly proclaimed.

Ninth, when you find that the Word of God renews you, and begins to be more precious to you than formerly when you heard the doctrines of men, then you may be sure that this is the work of God within you.

Tenth, when you find that it gives you assurance of the grace of God and eternal salvation, it is of God.

Eleventh, when you find that it crushes and destroys you, but magnifies God himself within you, it is a work of God.

Twelfth, when you find that the fear of God begins to give you joy rather than sorrow, it is a sure working of the Word and Spirit of God. May God grant us that Spirit. Amen.[3]

The big problem

The key underlying issue is that the primary obstacle to good hermeneutics is not a failure to read a text in context or identify its genre. Indeed, these, we might argue, are all symptoms of a more fundamental problem: human sin.

The fool who says in his heart there is no God is not *intellectually* bankrupt. Their problem is not that they've failed to read enough theology or take enough courses in hermeneutics. Their problem is that they're *morally* bankrupt:

> The fool says in his heart,
>   'There is no God.'

> They are corrupt, their deeds are vile;
>> there is no one who does good.
> (Psalm 14:1)

Paul expands on this in Romans 1:18–25. What may be known about God is 'plain'. 'For since the creation of the world God's invisible qualities – his eternal power and divine nature – have been clearly seen, being understood from what has been made, so that people are without excuse' (verse 20). The problem is that people 'suppress the truth by their wickedness' (verse 18). 'Their thinking became futile and their foolish hearts were darkened' (verse 21). And the reason for this is: 'Although they knew God, they neither glorified him as God nor gave thanks to him' (verse 21). We refuse to recognize God's authority (by worshipping him), and we refuse to recognize our dependence (by being grateful).

What this means is that we all readily find reasons for doing what we want to do. You've probably experienced this for yourself if you've ever talked through a decision with individuals who have already made up their mind. They amplify every point in favour of what they want to do and dismiss each point against. A conversation like that is a kind of exposé of what's going on in the human heart all the time.

We like to think of ourselves as rational beings who make cool, calculated decisions. But at the most fundamental level, we do what we want to do and then find reasons for doing it. We follow the desires of our hearts. Our desires control our reason. Proverbs 4:23 says,

> Above all else, guard your heart,
>> for everything you do flows from it.

Everything flows from the desires of your heart.

Think about what this means when we read the Bible. If we're finding reasons to do what we want, how will we read the Bible? We'll be constantly ignoring it, distorting it, twisting it, evading it. We will do mental gymnastics to avoid any challenge to the desires of our hearts. It's telling that most Christians are happy to accept the authority of the Bible until it teaches something they don't like. It rather gives the game away. The underlying issue is not whether the Bible is God's word, but whether we'll obey it – and therefore him.

We filter the Bible's teaching through what seems reasonable. We filter it through what other Christians do. Or we use some otherwise perfectly good hermeneutical tools – like reading the Bible in its cultural or historical context – in order to make it mean less or more than it actually means. John Webster says,

> We do not read well, not only because of technical incompetence, cultural distance from the substance of the text or lack of readerly sophistication, but also and most of all because in reading Scripture we are addressed by that which runs clean counter to our will. Reading Scripture is thus a moral matter; it requires that we become certain kinds of readers, whose reading is taken up into the history of reconciliation.[4]

Occasionally I catch myself doing this consciously. I find myself thinking, 'It can't mean that because the implications are too big for me to live with.' But moments like that are just the tip of the iceberg. Much more often I *subconsciously* make the Bible say more than it says or less than it says. Why? Because I want to justify my desires and actions. We are always at the job of self-justification. And too often we use the Bible to help us.

Dying to read the Bible

This means that death and resurrection need to shape how we approach the Bible:

- We need to come to the Bible in repentance and humility, putting sin to death, examining our prejudices, asking God to expose our selfish desires and pride, submitting our lives to God's will, trembling before God's word.
- We need to come to the Bible in anticipation and prayer, expecting the Spirit to reveal Christ, looking to the word to bring life, listening for God's voice, praying for comfort, assurance and hope.

Think about the words we often use to describe our interaction with the Bible. We talk about *grappling* with the text or *grasping* the meaning of a verse. We *get hold* of the meaning or *apprehend* it. We try to *get a handle on* a passage or *come to terms* with it. We *catch, capture* and *seize* an idea. It's all aggressive language. They're all words that imply control. It's not wrong to use this kind of language. It's metaphorical. But it can reflect and reinforce a dangerous attitude towards the Bible. Our job, we assume, is to master the text. But that's to get things the wrong way round. It's the job of the Bible to master us. Our responsibility is to be mastered by the text. God rules through his word, and we're to submit to his rule. That's why we come to the Bible trembling. We come as subjects before the King of heaven. John Webster says a true reading of Scripture 'can only occur as a kind of brokenness, a relinquishment of willed mastery of the text'.[5]

If we return to the Bible's own hermeneutical principles, we find verses such as: 'Before I was afflicted I went astray, but now I obey your word' (Psalm 119:67); 'It was good for me to be afflicted so that I might learn your decrees' (Psalm 119:71). Only those who have come to an end of their own wisdom, power and goodness are open to see the glory of God in the cross.

Or consider the words of Jesus in John 7:17: 'Anyone who chooses to do the will of God will find out whether my teaching comes from God or whether I speak on my own.' What's the key to recognizing the teaching of Jesus as the word of God? Submission to the will of God. In the parable of the sower, Jesus says that what prevents people hearing the word in a fruitful way is the work of the devil, the threat of persecution (which will include a desire for cultural conformity) and 'life's worries, riches and pleasures'. The requirement for fruitful hearing is 'a noble and good heart' (Luke 8:11–15).

Renewed readers

Reading the Bible, says Webster, is part of 'the fundamental pattern of all Christian existence, which is dying and rising with Jesus Christ through the purging and quickening power of the Holy Spirit'.

We come to the Bible doubting ourselves or mistrusting ourselves. That is, we come all too aware of our tendency to twist the Bible to justify ourselves. But alongside this brokenness is the expectation that the Holy Spirit will reveal Christ in the Bible and give life through the Bible. That means we can come with confidence.

This is just as important. Without dying to self, we'll become *presumptuous* readers. And without the life-giving Spirit, we'll become *hesitant* readers. But we have no reason to be hesitant. We come trusting in the Holy Spirit. As a result, we're confident that as we read the Bible, we'll hear the voice of God. We'll understand more of the truth. We'll be renewed, refreshed and restored.

What we're talking about here is primarily an *attitude* to the Bible, including:

- *repentance and faith:* repenting of our selfish desires and pride alongside faith in the light-giving and life-giving work of the Spirit;
- *humility and confidence:* humbly submitting to God's will and wisdom alongside confidence in God's word and Spirit;
- *mistrust and trust:* mistrusting our tendency towards self-justification alongside a trust in the word and Spirit to cut through our self-deceit with divine truth.

But there are ways of embedding these *attitudes* in our *practices.*

Charles E. Hambrick-Stowe traces the pattern of death and resurrection in the practice of Puritan spirituality. In *The Practice of Piety* he uses sermons, diaries and devotional manuals to build up a picture of the day-to-day piety of ordinary Christians and churches. In other words, he looks at what they did in practice and not just what they said in theory. This is what Hambrick-Stowe concludes about Puritan spirituality:

> The pattern of spiritual stages first established in conversion
> continued to mark the journey to heaven. The devotional
> life of the saints, the means by which they progressed
> on the pilgrimage, was a system of ritual self-emptying
> in preparation for the renewed experience of being filled
> by God with his grace. The redemptive cycle of Christ's
> death and resurrection was translated into a set of spiritual

exercises, devotional acts that became the path of renewed repentance and fulfilment.[6]

The spiritual dynamics of preparation and implantation – death and resurrection, repentance for sin and subsequent salvation – described the actual experience of individuals over the course of their spiritual lives . . . The redemptive cycle of death and resurrection was an element in the very air New Englanders breathed, unavoidable and ubiquitous in the rituals of public worship and the words of private devotion.[7]

What might this look like?

1. Pray before you read the word

When you read the Bible on your own or when you study it in a group, begin with prayer. I realize you probably do this already. My aim is that you would do it with a new conviction and a new meaning. Don't let it become perfunctory or notional. We can't read the Bible on our own. Left to our selfish selves, we'll twist it into something that serves our purposes. We need God's help.

2. Repent as you read the word

It's all too easy to come to the Bible looking to have our prejudices confirmed. Think 'trembling'! Ask yourself, 'Am I trembling before God's word?' Come to the Bible actively conscious of the need to submit your thinking, desires and will to God's word. Come to be mastered by God and not to master the text.

3. Prepare to hear the word preached

The Puritans typically used to have a time of repentance on a Saturday night in readiness to hear God's life-giving, grace-filled word the next day. They went through the process of death and resurrection, repentance and faith, each week as they prepared to hear, and then heard, the word being preached.

4. Repent as you hear the word preached

It's very tempting to evade the judging and exposing work of God's word. Here are a couple of 'tactics' to avoid.

First, apply it to someone else. Have you ever sat during a sermon thinking something like this? 'I'm so glad so-and-so is here to hear this message. He really needs to hear this. I hope he's squirming.' By applying the word to someone else in this way, you're failing to apply it to yourself. By all means, think about how you might talk through the sermon with someone in the coming week to build that person up. But apply the message to yourself first.

Second, evaluate the preacher. We need to listen to sermons with discernment, subjecting them to the ultimate authority of God's word. But the greater danger for most of us is listening to sermons with a critical spirit. We pick over the fine details of the exegesis or style. We evaluate the preacher rather than allowing ourselves to be evaluated by God's word. We become 'pundits' rather than servants.

5. Read the Bible in community

We're often blind to our sin and the way we use the Bible to justify ourselves. We need other people to highlight our sin and misunderstandings. So we need to read the Bible as part of a community who will graciously challenge our thinking and behaviour. It's wise and humble to start with the assumption that your pastor, church and church tradition have understood the Bible better than you have. Scripture alone means we're willing to set aside tradition; the communion of saints means we hesitate before doing so.

It's also very easy for us to read the Bible as if it's written to *me* as an individual. But first and foremost, it's written to *us* as the people of God. So the Bible is constantly reminding me that I need to see myself as part of a wider community. I find myself in giving myself in love to God and to others.

In Ephesians 4, Paul describes how Christians grow towards maturity through 'knowledge of the Son of God' (verse 13). But he also emphasizes that we do this *together* as we 'speak the truth in love' to one another (verse 15). It's often other Christians who point out our selfish desires. Or those selfish desires hide dormant until provoked by other people. Living life together in community allows for that to happen.

At a church gathering on a Sunday morning everyone looks happy, sorted, faithful. Everyone looks like a wonderful model of godliness. But when the kids are arguing or the car's broken down or you're running late – that's when our true selves are revealed. And that's when other Christians can speak the truth to us in love. We need to read the Bible with people who know us enough and love us enough to speak the truth to us. We're to be communities in which we encourage, challenge, console, rebuke, counsel, exhort and comfort one another with the truth:

These are the ones I look on with favour:
  those who are humble and contrite in spirit,
  and who tremble at my word.
(Isaiah 66:2)

Come, let us return to the LORD.
He has torn us to pieces
  but he will heal us;
he has injured us
  but he will bind up our wounds.
(Hosea 6:1)

Conclusion

Why I love the Bible

Why do I love the Bible? I can't put it better than William Tyndale. In 1526 Tyndale published the New Testament in English. It was his second attempt to do so. First time round he'd had to flee when the authorities raided the press on which it was being printed. He was living in exile and would eventually be martyred for his passion to make an English Bible available to every ploughboy in the land. He included a preface to that first edition which he later expanded into *A Pathway into the Holy Scripture*. Here's what he said about the gospel and the Bible:

> Evangelion (what we call 'the gospel') is a Greek word; and signifies good, merry, glad and joyful tidings, that make a man's heart glad, and make him sing, dance, and leap for joy. When David had killed Goliath the giant, glad tidings came to the Jews, that their fearful and cruel enemy was slain, and they were delivered out of all danger. Because of this gladness, they sung, danced and were joyful. In the same way the Evangelion of God (which we call the Gospel and the New Testament) is the

joyful tidings, published by the apostles throughout all the world, of Christ the true David. It tells how he has fought with sin, with death, and the devil, and overcome them. Whereby all men that were in bondage to sin, wounded with death, overcome by the devil, are without their own merits or deservings, loosed, justified, restored to life, and saved, brought to liberty, and reconciled to the favour of God, and set at one with him again. As many as believe these tidings laud, praise and thank God, and are glad, sing and dance for joy.

This Evangelion or Gospel (that is to say, such joyful tidings) is called the New Testament. That's because when a man dies he appoints his goods to be dealt and distributed after his death among them which he names to be his heirs [in his last will and testament]. In the same way Christ before his death commanded and appointed that such evangelion, gospel or tidings should be declared throughout all the world, and thereby to give to all that believe all his goods, that is to say: his life, through which he swallowed and devoured up death; his righteousness, through which he banished sin; his salvation, through which he overcame eternal damnation. Now can the wretched man (that is wrapped in sin, and is in danger to death and hell) hear no more joyous a thing, than such glad and comfortable tidings of Christ. So he cannot but be glad and laugh from the low bottom of his heart, if he believe that the tidings are true.

To strengthen such faith, God promised this, his Evangelion, in the Old Testament by the prophets . . . In the Old Testament are many promises, which are nothing else but the Evangelion or gospel, to save those that believed from the vengeance of the law.[1]

What's the Bible? It is good, merry, glad and joyful tidings.

Why? Because it tells how Christ has overcome sin, death and the devil. It tells how those in bondage to sin, wounded with death and overcome by the devil have been set free by Christ. It tells how we're restored to life, brought to liberty and reconciled to God.

How should we respond? We cannot but be glad and laugh from the very bottom of our hearts. We praise and thank God. We're glad, sing and dance for joy. There are only two times when I dance: when I'm with small children, and alone in my study when God's word grabs my heart.

Why do I love the Bible? Because it's full of the good news of the gospel. Because it's full of the glory of God. Because it's full of the grace of Jesus. Because it fizzes with the power of the Spirit. Because whenever I open it, I do so with excited expectation. In its pages I find comfort, challenge, instruction, wisdom, joy, grace, glory.

There have been many times when I've read my Bible and nothing has happened. I've not felt informed or blessed or comforted. I've read the words, closed my Bible and got on with the day. I still believe on those days that it's at work in my life.

But there have also been many times when I've met God in his word.

O Lord our Rock

The following setting of Psalm 19:7–14 embodies the truths of this book. I've written the lyrics, and my friend Rob Spink has composed a tune. There's a recording at http://thehousebandmusic.bandcamp.com/track/o-lord-our-rock and a lead sheet at http://thecrowdedhouse.org/music.

O Lord our Rock, redeeming King,
your truth alone can comfort bring
when we are in distress.
Your perfect law revives the soul
and binds our wounds and makes us whole,
your promise leads to rest.

Your precepts make our hearts rejoice
for in your word we hear your voice,
the voice of God above.
Your gospel breaks like break of day
to give us light to light our way,
to walk in paths of love.

Your statutes make your people wise,
illuminating darkened eyes
for your commands are true.
Your word is firm and will endure.
The fear that it evokes is pure
and binds our hearts to you.

Your word is worth far more than gold
for in its pages we behold
the treasury of Christ.
Its lines upon the tongue are sweet:
they lead us to our Saviour's feet
and his great sacrifice.

As your decrees are read and taught,
may every word and every thought
be pleasing to you, Lord.
Your Spirit's power to all impart
that Christ may dwell in every heart,
and be our true reward.

May wand'ring hearts be warned from sin,
may troubled souls find peace within,
may Christ be our delight.
Forgive our faults, unlock our chains,
and in our lives restore your reign:
our hearts with love ignite.[1]

Notes

1. The God who speaks

1. George Robinson (1838–1877), 'Loved with Everlasting Love'.
2. B. B. Warfield, 'The Real Problem of Inspiration', in Peter A. Lillback and Richard B. Gaffin Jr (eds.), *Thy Word Is Still Truth: Essential Writings on the Doctrine of Scripture from the Reformation to Today* (P&R, 2013), p. 859.
3. Francis Turretin, *Institutes of Elenctic Theology* (P&R, 1992), 1.58.
4. At https://www.ccel.org/creeds/helvetic.htm, emphasis added.
5. Martin Luther, 'Sermons on the Gospel of St. John', *Luther's Works*, vol. 22 (Concordia, 1968), pp. 526–527.
6. John Calvin, comments on Isaiah 11:4, *Calvin's Commentaries: Isaiah* (AP&A), p. 175.
7. William Perkins, *Cases of Conscience*, in *Works*, vol. 2 (John Legatt, 1631), pp. 70–71.

2. God spoke in the Bible

1. See B. B. Warfield, 'Inspiration', in *Revelation and Inspiration* (Baker, 2003), p. 79.

2. J. I. Packer, *'Fundamentalism' and the Word of God* (IVF, 1958), p. 81.

3. See John A. Woodbridge, *Biblical Authority* (Zondervan, 1982); G. W. Bromiley, 'The Church Fathers and Holy Scripture', in D. A. Carson and John A. Woodbridge (eds.), *Scripture and Truth* (IVP, 1983).

3. God speaks in the Bible

1. Cited in B. Godfrey Buxton, *The Reward of Faith in the Life of Barclay F. Buxton* (Japan Evangelistic Band, 1949), p. 263.

2. Henry Walter (ed.), *Works of William Tyndale*, Parker Society, 1848–1850 (Banner of Truth, 2010), 1.400.

4. God speaks Jesus in the Bible

1. Irenaeus, *Against Heresies*, 4.26.1.

2. Tim Chester, *From Creation to New Creation: Understanding the Bible Story*, 2nd edn (The Good Book Company, 2010).

3. John Stott, *Basic Christianity* (IVP, 2013).

4. See http://www.ceministries.org.

5. See chapters 4 and 5 of Tim Chester, *Mission Matters* (IVP, 2015).

5. The Bible is relational

1. Timothy Ward, *Words of Life: Scripture as the Living and Active Word of God* (IVP, 2009), p. 32.

2. John Calvin, *Institutes of the Christian Religion*, ed. J. T. McNeill, trans. F. L. Battles, Library of Christian Classics, vols. XX and XXI (Westminster, 1960), 2.9.3 and 3.2.6.

3. John White, *A Way to the Tree of Life: Discoursed in Sundry Directions for the Profitable Reading of the Scriptures*, cited in Charles E. Hambrick-Stowe, *The Practice of Piety: Puritan Devotional Principles in Puritan New England* (University of North Carolina Press, 1982), p. 159.

4. John Calvin, sermon on Ephesians 4:11–12, in *Sermons on the Epistle to the Ephesians* (Banner of Truth, 1973), p. 368.

5. Henry Walter (ed.), *Works of William Tyndale*, Parker Society, 1848–1850 (Banner of Truth, 2010), 1.160.

6. John M. Frame, *The Doctrine of the Word of God* (P&R, 2010), p. 63.

7. Augustine, *On Christian Doctrine*, 1.35, *Nicene and Post-Nicene Fathers*, Series 1, vol. 2, ed. Philip Schaff (Hendrickson, 1994), pp. 532–533.

6. The Bible is intentional

1. Peter Jensen, *The Revelation of God* (IVP, 2002), p. 93.

2. Timothy Ward, *Words of Life: Scripture as the Living and Active Word of God* (IVP, 2009), pp. 174–175.

3. Kevin Vanhoozer, *The Drama of Doctrine* (Westminster John Knox, 2005), p. 210.

7. The Bible is enough

1. Andrew Wilson, *Unbreakable: What the Son of God Said about the Word of God* (10Publishing, 2014), p. 25.

2. Peter Adam, *Written for Us: Receiving God's Words in the Bible* (IVP, 2008), pp. 122–123.

8. The Bible is reliable

1. John M. Frame, *The Doctrine of the Word of God* (P&R, 2010), p. 537.

2. David Shaw, 'Mapping the Debate: The Doctrine of Scripture in Our Contemporary Context', *True to His Word*, Primer, vol. 1 (FIEC, 2015), p. 22.

3. Daniel Strange and Michael Ovey, *Confident: Why We Can Trust the Bible* (Christian Focus, 2015), p. 41.

4. Tim Keller, *The Reason for God* (Hodder & Stoughton, 2008), p. 114.

5. Peter Jensen, *The Revelation of God* (IVP, 2002), p. 42.
6. C. S. Lewis, 'Is Theology Poetry?', *Essay Collection and Other Short Pieces* (HarperCollins, 2000), p. 21.
7. John Owen, *The Divine Origin of the Scriptures*, in *Works*, ed. William Goold, vol. 16 (T. & T. Clark, 1862), pp. 319–322.
8. Ibid., p. 322.
9. Charles H. Spurgeon, in a sermon entitled 'Christ and His Co-Workers', 10 June 1886. Cited in *True to His Word*, Primer, vol. 1 (FIEC, 2015), p. 5.

9. The Bible is accessible

1. The Westminster Confession of Faith, 1.7, www.reformed. org/documents/wcf_with_proofs/index.html?body=/ documents/wcf_with_proofs/ch_I.html.
2. Erasmus, 'On the Freedom of the Will', in E. Gordon Rupp and Philip S. Watson (eds.), *Luther and Erasmus*, Library of Christian Classics, vol. XVII (SCM/Westminster, 1969), p. 43.
3. Ibid., p. 44.
4. Ibid., p. 40.
5. Martin Luther, 'On the Bondage of the Will', in E. Gordon Rupp and Philip S. Watson (eds.), *Luther and Erasmus*, Library of Christian Classics, vol. XVII (SCM/Westminster, 1969), p. 110.
6. Ibid., p. 162.
7. Ibid., p. 112.
8. Ibid., p. 162.
9. Mark Thompson, 'The Generous Gift of a Gracious Father: Toward a Theological Account of the Clarity of Scripture', in D. A. Carson (ed.), *The Enduring Authority of the Christian Scriptures* (Eerdmans, 2016), p. 616.
10. Martin Luther, 'On the Bondage of the Will', in E. Gordon Rupp and Philip S. Watson (eds.), *Luther and Erasmus*, Library of Christian Classics, vol. XVII (SCM/Westminster, 1969), p. 111.

11. Huldrych Zwingli, 'The Clarity and Certainty of the Word of God', in G. W. Bromiley (ed.), *Zwingli and Bullinger*, Library of Christian Classics (Westminster Kohn Knox Press, 1953), p. 87.

10. Dying to read the Bible

1. John Calvin, *Institutes of the Christian Religion*, ed. J. T. McNeill, trans. F. L. Battles, Library of Christian Classics, vols. XX and XXI (Westminster, 1960), 3.3.1–9.
2. I owe this suggestion to Marcus Honeysett, Director of Living Leadership (www.livingleadership.org).
3. Huldrych Zwingli, 'The Clarity and Certainty of the Word of God,' in G. W. Bromiley (ed.), *Zwingli and Bullinger*, Library of Christian Classics (Westminster John Knox Press, 1953), pp. 93–95.
4. John Webster, *Holy Scripture: A Dogmatic Sketch* (CUP, 2003), pp. 81–86.
5. Ibid., pp. 81–86.
6. Charles E. Hambrick-Stowe, *The Practice of Piety: Puritan Devotional Principles in Puritan New England* (University of North Carolina Press, 1982), pp. 89–90.
7. Ibid., p. 21.

Conclusion: Why I love the Bible

1. Henry Walter (ed.), *Works of William Tyndale*, Parker Society, 1848–1850 (Banner of Truth, 2010), 1.8–9, 11. I have made minor changes to update the language and punctuation.

O Lord our Rock

1. Words © Tim Chester 2014. Music © Rob Spink 2014.

Further reading

The books selected here suggest some next steps if you want to explore the ideas in this book further. They're listed in order in each category, from easy-to-read to more challenging.

Three books on the Bible

Tim Ward, *Words of Life: Scripture as the Living and Active Word of God* (IVP, 2009).
Peter Adam, *Written for Us: Receiving God's Words in the Bible* (IVP, 2008).
John Webster, *Holy Scripture: A Dogmatic Sketch* (CUP, 2003).

Three books on how to understand the Bible

Nigel Beynon and Andrew Sach, *Dig Deeper: Tools to Unearth the Bible's Treasure* (IVP, 2010).
J. Scott Duvall and J. Daniel Hays, *Grasping God's Word* (Zondervan, 2012).
Peter J. Leithart, *Deep Exegesis: The Mystery of Reading Scripture* (Baylor, 2009).

Three books on seeing Christ in the whole Bible

Tim Chester, *From Creation to New Creation* (The Good Book Company, 2010).
Vaughan Roberts, *God's Big Picture* (IVP, 2004).
Graeme Goldsworthy, *According to Plan: The Unfolding Revelation of God in the Bible* (IVP, 1991).

Three books on defending the Bible

Barry Cooper, *Can I Really Trust the Bible?* (The Good Book Company, 2014).
Daniel Strange and Michael Ovey, *Confident: Why We Can Trust the Bible* (Christian Focus, 2015).
John Piper, *A Peculiar Glory: How the Christian Scriptures Reveal Their Complete Truthfulness* (IVP, 2016).

Three really big books on the Bible

John M. Frame, *The Doctrine of the Word of God* (P&R, 2010).
D. A. Carson (ed.), *The Enduring Authority of the Christian Scriptures* (Apollos, 2016).
Peter A. Lillback and Richard B. Gaffin Jr, *Thy Word Is Still Truth: Essential Writings on the Doctrine of Scripture from the Reformation to Today* (P&R, 2013).

KESWICK MINISTRIES

Our purpose
Keswick Ministries is committed to the spiritual renewal of God's people for his mission in the world.

God's purpose is to bring his blessing to all the nations of the world. That promise of blessing, which touches every aspect of human life, is ultimately fulfilled through the life, death, resurrection, ascension and future return of Christ. All of the people of God are called to participate in his missionary purposes, wherever he may place them. The central vision of Keswick Ministries is to see the people of God equipped, encouraged and refreshed to fulfil that calling, directed and guided by God's Word in the power of his Spirit, for the glory of his Son.

Our priorities
Keswick Ministries seeks to serve the local church through:

- **Hearing God's Word**: the Scriptures are the foundation for the church's life, growth and mission, and Keswick Ministries is committed to preach and teach God's Word in a way that is faithful to Scripture and relevant to Christians of all ages and backgrounds.
- **Becoming like God's Son**: from its earliest days the Keswick movement has encouraged Christians to live godly lives in the power of the Spirit, to grow in Christlikeness and to live under his lordship in every area of life. This is God's will for his people in every culture and generation.
- **Serving God's mission**: the authentic response to God's Word is obedience to his mission, and the inevitable result of Christlikeness is sacrificial service. Keswick

Ministries seeks to encourage committed discipleship in family life, work and society, and energetic engagement in the cause of world mission.

Our ministry

- **Keswick: the event**. Every summer the town of Keswick hosts a three-week Convention, which attracts some 15,000 Christians from the UK and around the world. The event provides Bible teaching for all ages, vibrant worship, a sense of unity across generations and denominations, and an inspirational call to serve Christ in the world. It caters for children of all ages and has a strong youth and young adult programme. And it all takes place in the beautiful Lake District – a perfect setting for rest, recreation and refreshment.
- **Keswick: the movement**. For 140 years the work of Keswick has impacted churches worldwide, and today the movement is underway throughout the UK, as well as in many parts of Europe, Asia, North America, Australia, Africa and the Caribbean. Keswick Ministries is committed to strengthen the network in the UK and beyond, through prayer, news, pioneering and cooperative activity.
- **Keswick resources**. Keswick Ministries is producing a growing range of books and booklets based on the core foundations of Christian life and mission. It makes Bible teaching available through free access to mp3 downloads, and the sale of DVDs and CDs. It broadcasts online through Clayton TV and annual BBC Radio 4 services. In addition to the summer Convention, Keswick Ministries is hoping to develop other teaching and training events in the coming years.

Our unity

The Keswick movement worldwide has adopted a key Pauline statement to describe its gospel inclusivity: 'for you are all one in Christ Jesus' (Galatians 3:28). Keswick Ministries works with evangelicals from a wide variety of church backgrounds, on the understanding that they share a commitment to the essential truths of the Christian faith as set out in our statement of belief.

Our contact details

Mail: Keswick Ministries, Keswick Convention Centre, Skiddaw Street, Keswick, CA12 4BY, England
T: 017687 80075
E: info@keswickministries.org
W: www.keswickministries.org

related titles from IVP

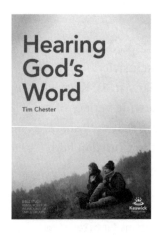

KESWICK STUDY GUIDE

Hearing God's Word
Tim Chester

ISBN: 978–1–78359–581–5
80 pages, paperback

What has God said? How has he said it? And how does it apply to our lives today?

Hearing God's Word invites us to explore these questions and more.

Each session starts with an introduction to the topic and then moves to a Bible passage. We focus on the theme, go deeper and explore living out the word in our daily lives. Useful prayer prompts also help to make the message deep, real and personal.

'Biblical, practical, devotional and thoughtful. An excellent resource for group or personal study to strengthen our convictions about the truth of the Bible, and enable us to discover its riches for ourselves.' John Risbridger

'Here is a workable, practical guide that will help you to study the Bible by yourself or with others. Used well, it will help you grow in your faith.' Ian Coffey

Available from your local Christian bookshop or **www.ivpbooks.com**

related titles from IVP

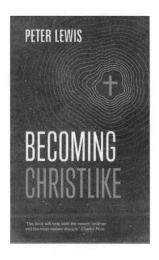

FROM THE KESWICK FOUNDATIONS SERIES

Becoming Christlike

Peter Lewis

ISBN: 978–1–78359–437–5

192 pages, paperback

'God wants his people to become like Christ,' said international preacher, writer and teacher John Stott in a public address at the end of his long life.

Peter Lewis is similarly passionate about the Bible's message – that God has a plan that centres on Jesus and includes each one of us.

In this helpful and accessible book, he focuses on

- the source of Christlikeness
- the model of Christlikeness
- the helps to Christlikeness
- the contradictions to Christlikeness
- the triumphs of Christlikeness

Here, the reader who wants to become like Christ will find radical – sometimes challenging – teaching, practical wisdom and reassurance.

'Clear, compelling, biblically rich, and full of sparkling stories and meaningful quotes . . . I couldn't put this book down.' Becky Manley Pippert

Available from your local Christian bookshop or **www.ivpbooks.com**

related titles from IVP

FROM THE KESWICK FOUNDATIONS SERIES

Discipleship Matters
Dying to Live for Christ
Peter Maiden

ISBN: 978–1–78359–355–2

160 pages, paperback

Discipleship involves a gentle journey with our Saviour. Its demands will dovetail happily with our carefully crafted plans.

Wrong. Peter Maiden pulls no punches as he focuses on what a disciple should look like today. Are we prepared to follow Jesus' example, to lose our lives for his sake? Are we willing to live counter-culturally in a world that values power, prestige and money, and constantly puts self at the centre?

Of all people, Jesus, the Son of God, has the authority to require this of us. And he's calling us to a relationship, not to a set of rules or a miserable, spartan existence. In fact, it is through losing our lives that we find them, and thereby discover the source of pure joy.

What a pity we set the bar too low.

'Engagingly personal and resolutely biblical. A delight to read. But beware, it is also an exciting challenge.' Tim Chester

'Readable, practical, comprehensive in its scope and global in its vision . . . a call to authentic discipleship.' John Risbridger

Available from your local Christian bookshop or **www.ivpbooks.com**

related titles from IVP

FROM THE KESWICK FOUNDATIONS SERIES

Mission Matters
Love Says Go
Tim Chester

ISBN: 978–1–78359–280–7
176 pages, paperback

The Father delights in his Son.

This is the starting point of mission, its very core.

The word 'mission' means 'sending'. But for many centuries this was only used to describe what God did, sending his Son and his Spirit into the world.

World mission exists because the Father wants people to delight in his Son, and the Son wants people to delight in the Father.

Tim Chester introduces us to a cascade of love: love flowing from the Father to the Son through the Spirit. And that love overflows and, through us, keeps on flowing to our Christian community and beyond, to a needy world.

Mission matters. This book is for ordinary individuals willing to step out and be part of the most amazing, exciting venture in the history of the world.

Available from your local Christian bookshop or **www.ivpbooks.com**

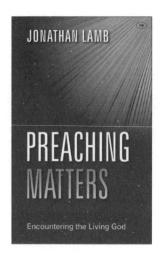

related titles from IVP

FROM THE KESWICK FOUNDATIONS SERIES

Preaching Matters
Encountering the Living God
Jonathan Lamb

ISBN: 978–1–78359–149–7

192 pages, paperback

Preaching matters. It is a God-ordained means of encountering Christ. This is happening all around the world. The author recalls the student who, on hearing a sermon about new life in Christ, found faith that changed his life for ever; and the couple facing the trauma of the wife's terminal illness who discovered that Christ was all they needed, following a sermon on Habakkuk.

When the Bible is faithfully and relevantly explained, it transforms hearts, understandings and attitudes. Most of all, it draws us into a living relationship with God through Christ.

This is a book to ignite our passion for preaching, whether we preach every week or have no idea how to put a sermon together. It will encourage every listener to participate in the dynamic event of God's word speaking to his people through his Holy Spirit. God's word is dynamite; little wonder that its effects are often dynamic.

'A book for both preachers and listeners . . . a fitting manifesto not just for the Keswick Convention, but for every local church.' Tim Chester

Available from your local Christian bookshop or **www.ivpbooks.com**